P. C. Alexander's was a vantage view of Indira Gandhi's prime ministership from 1981 till her assassination and Rajiv Gandhi's taking over as Prime Minister in October 1984. During this period he served as Mrs Gandhi's Principal Secretary, involved by her own wishes, not only in government affairs but also in her party, political, and sometimes, personal matters. It is thus an important and honest insider's account of much of what happened during that period, including:

♦ the rocky shoals through which her relations had to pass with two successive Presidents
♦ new insights into Mrs Gandhi's role in the dismissals of the first communist government in Kerala in 1957, and N.T. Rama Rao's government in Andhra Pradesh in 1984
♦ the background on various cabinet reshuffles
♦ her assessment of key party and government colleagues
♦ her attitude towards those who had deserted her in her years out of power (1977-1980)
♦ how Mrs Gandhi seriously considered the possibility of contesting the Presidential election of 1982 and how she struck up an enduring political alliance with the hugely popular Chief Minister of Tamil Nadu, M. G. Ramachandran
♦ the major thrust Mrs Gandhi made in improving India's international relations
♦ Indira Gandhi's death and the drama behind Rajiv Gandhi's succession as Prime Minister.

Here, then, is a book which gives an insider's account of Indira Gandhi's second innings as India's Prime Minister.

It is rare for Indian civil servants to write about the events they have observed during their career. To quote Dr. Alexander, he has chosen to depart from this tradition because "I have been greatly impelled by sense of history and of duty to record the events relating to the most critical years of Indira Gandhi's life. I happened to have been the only witness to some of them..."

Dr. Padinjarethalakal Cherian Alexander was born in Kerala and studied History and Economics at the Travancore and Annamalai Universities. He joined the Indian Administrative Service in 1948 and rose to be Secretary, Foreign Trade and Commerce Secretary, after holding several important positions. He was trained at the Board of Trade, U.K. under a Nuffield Foundation Fellowship and was a research fellow at the Stanford

Research Institute, California under a Ford Foundation Fellowship.

Dr. Alexander was serving the International Trade Centre (UNCTAD-GATT) at Geneva when he was invited by Indira Gandhi in 1981 to join her Secretariat as her Principal Secretary. After Indira Gandhi's death, he continued to work with Rajiv Gandhi in the same capacity. He later served as High Commissioner for India in the U. K. (1985-88) and as Governor of Tamil Nadu during 1988-90.

Dr. Alexander is the author of three other books – *The Dutch in Malabar, Buddhism in Kerala* and *Industrial Estates in India.*

My years with Indira Gandhi

P.C. ALEXANDER

VISION BOOKS

(Incorporating Orient Paperbacks)

New Delhi • Mumbai • Hyderabad

www.visionbooksindia.com

First Published 1991
Reprinted 2001, 2002, 2003,
2005, 2006, 2009, 2012, 2018

ISBN 81-7094-442-2

Published by
Vision Books Pvt. Ltd.
(Incorporating Orient Paperbacks & CARING imprints)
24 Feroze Gandhi Road, Lajpat Nagar 3
New Delhi 110024 (India)
Phone: (+91-11) 2984 0821 / 22
e-mail: visionbooks@gmail.com

Printed at
Anand Sons
C-88, Ganesh Nagar, Pandav Nagar Complex
Delhi-110 092, India.

CONTENTS

PREFACE

I started working on this book about the middle of 1985 when the memory of my years with Indira Gandhi was still quite fresh. Pressure of work, however, allowed me to devote time to it only intermittently, and the book could be completed only now. Even though different parts of the book were written on different occasions, I have tried to maintain the continuity of the narrative, starting from the circumstances leading to my appointment as Principal Secretary and ending with 3 November 1984, when "that graceful face which was so familiar to every hamlet and household in India was consumed by sandalwood flames".

It is rare for Indian civil servants to write about the events they have observed during their career. I have chosen to depart from this tradition as I have been impelled by my sense of history and of duty to record the events relating to the most critical years of Indira Gandhi's life. I happened to have been the only witness to some of them and I thought I would be failing in my duty if I did not make them known to the public.

A book on my years with Indira Gandhi cannot be complete without an account of her handling of the Punjab problem. The text on this is ready and I had wanted to publish the book with the chapters on Punjab included in it. I have, however, decided to withhold these chapters for the present and hope to publish them as a sequel to this book when the situation in that State improves.

Condensed extracts from the rest of the book were published in the form of articles in some newspapers during August-November 1990. The response of readers was heartening and I received numerous requests for publication of the full text in book form. I hope this book will prove to be useful for a fair and proper understanding of Indira Gandhi's personality and style of working.

There were several occasions during the last five years when the pressures and strains of official work made me consider putting off completion of the book to a later date when I could hope to have less work and more leisure. But one person persistently urged me to finish the book as a duty which should not be postponed. That was my wife Ackama, herself an ardent admirer of Indira Gandhi. On this occasion, when the book is being placed before the public, I wish to gratefully acknowledge her very important role in ensuring its completion.

10 March 1991
Bangalore

P.C. ALEXANDER

1

MY APPOINTMENT

"Why did Indira Gandhi select you as her Principal Secretary? Did she know you so well?" – I have been asked these questions several times in India and abroad. My reply has always been that I myself do not know how I came to be chosen for this post. Normally, a person selected for such a sensitive appointment as this should have been one closely known to Indira Gandhi, and who enjoyed her personal trust. I could not claim any such privilege at the time of my appointment. There were a few senior civil servants in Delhi who were known to Indira Gandhi personally, either because they had served in her home district in Uttar Pradesh or had had opportunities of working in the ministries under her direct charge in Delhi. I had no such prior acquaintance with her. Nor had I the opportunity of coming to her personal notice even after I came to hold some important civil service posts in the central government. Unlike civil servants working in ministries such as External Affairs or Home, those like me working in ministries like Commerce and Industries had only limited opportunity for coming to the personal notice of the Prime Minister in their official work. Indira Gandhi, of course, knew me to the extent that any Prime Minister would have known a senior officer working in one of the important economic ministries in the central government. As Secretary in the ministry of Commerce, I had met the Prime Minister on a few occasions, but I could not claim the privilege of being one of those closely known to her.

I remember the surprise expressed by the wife of a high dignitary in Denmark where I was on a visit as a member of the Prime Minister's delegation in June 1983 on her knowing that I was a Christian by religion. I was seated next to her at a banquet hosted by the Prime Minister of that country in honour of Indira Gandhi. "How is it that you Hindus have a name like Alexander?" she asked me looking at the name card in front of me. I explained to her that I did not know of any Hindu with Alexander as his surname, but there were many Christians in India with names like mine. I added that in Kerala, the southernmost State of India from where I came, there were over five million Christians and that the Christian population in India was over seventeen million. I also told her that I belonged to a church which claimed its origin to St Thomas the Apostle and that we had been Christians long before most European countries had known of Christianity. I said that names such as Alexander, Thomas, John and Mathew were very common among the Christians of Kerala.

What surprised her then was not the fact that I had a Christian ancestry going back to Apostolic times or that the Christians in India numbered more than thrice the total population of her own country, but the fact that Indira Gandhi had selected a Christian from Kerala as her Principal Secretary. In fact, several others in western countries had expressed surprise that Indira Gandhi had chosen as her Principal Secretary a person not belonging to her State, region or religion, which most political leaders tend to do. Since I never had the opportunity of working directly with her before, her knowledge about me was mainly through official records or reports. In fact, at the time of my selection to this post I was not even working for the Government of India. I had already opted for retirement from government service and was working as the head of the International Trade Center, UNCTAD, GATT (ITC), a United Nations Organisation located in Geneva.

Here, I should explain in some detail the background of my joining the UN service at Geneva as this has some relevance to my decision to accept the offer of appointment. The Executive Directorship of ITC was the third UN assignment in my career and I should start with an account of my three assignments with the UN to give a background about my outlook and philosophy regarding service in my own country and service with the United Nations. I should also narrate my own experiences of working under the Janata government as they are very relevant to the decision I took to leave the government and join the ITC.

First UN assignment

My first UN assignment was during 1963-66 when I worked as Senior Adviser at the Center for Industrial Development at the

United Nations Headquarters, New York. Prior to my selection to this post, I was working as Development Commissioner, Small Scale Industries, a post to which I was appointed in 1960 by Lal Bahadur Shastri, then Minister for Commerce and Industry, quite ahead of my entitlement, and overlooking the rules of seniority for promotion in the Indian Administrative Service, of which I was a member.

Those were the early days of the small industries development programme and several new programmes were being introduced in India which had attracted international attention. Industrial estates were one such programme. Early in 1963, the Economic Committee for Asia and Far East (ECAFE, now ESCAP) and the UN Center for Industrial Development jointly organised an international seminar on Industrial Estates at Madras. As Development Commissioner, I was nominated as leader of the twenty strong Indian delegation, to the seminar and following the conventions of international seminars, I, as leader of the host country's delegation, was elected as chairman of the seminar. The senior UN officials from New York who participated in the seminar somehow were impressed by my performance as chairman and my "expertise" in the subject and within a few days of their returning to New York sent me a telegram offering me the post of Adviser, Small Scale Industries and Industrial Estates at the UN headquarters. The terms were quite attractive and the prospect of living in New York tempting, but I was really in a dilemma as to what to do. Having received an out-of-turn promotion, I did not want to be misunderstood as having used my position to look for greener pastures. My doubts and reservations were, however, quickly resolved by the Secretary of my Ministry, S.Ranganathan, whose advice I sought about the UN offer. In a couple of minutes, he made the decision for me saying: "Look, you have not sought this job, but the job has come seeking you. While this is a tribute to you personally, it is also a recognition of the Indian programme and you should straightaway accept it''. That settled it, and in October 1963 I started working as an international civil servant.

However, after about two years with the UN, I began missing what is now called "job satisfaction" in my UN work. In India, I was responsible as Development Commissioner, for giving shape and direction to a programme of great national importance and I started feeling that I was wasting whatever experience and abilities

I had in return for a handsome pay packet. I missed the thrill and excitement of working for my own country and wanted to get back to Government of India service. K.B. Lall, who had been my senior colleague in the Commerce and Industries Ministry was Ambassador to the European Economic Community at Brussels at that time, and during a visit to New York he told me that he was returning to India as Commerce Secretary and would be very glad to have me as a Joint Secretary in his ministry if I decided to return. I promptly submitted my letter of resignation to the UN authorities and by October 1966, I was back in the Commerce ministry as Joint Secretary working with Lall.

Second UN assignment

I thought I had left UN service for good but very soon fate conspired to take me back to the UN again – this time as Chief of a UN project for Industrial Development in Teheran.

When I was working as Senior Adviser at the Center for Industrial Development in New York, I had led a Technical Assistance Mission to Teheran and formulated a project for reorganising their Industrial Estate complex at Ahwaz. The Government of Iran took three years to take a final decision on my recommendations, but when they decided to go ahead with the project on the lines recommended by me, they also informed the UN that they would do so only if the UN could arrange to secure my services as the head of the UN project team.

Those were the early days of Indo-Iranian economic co-operation and the governments of both the countries had been attaching a good deal of importance to the strengthening of such ties. There were strong pressures on the Government of India from both the Government of Iran and the UN for my services and even though I was most reluctant to take up another UN assignment, and that too in a place like Iran, I had to accept it and I joined as Chief of the UN project and Chief Adviser to the Government of Iran on Small Industries and Industrial Estates in January 1970.

The period 1970-73, when I was in Iran, saw the heyday of the Shah's rule. Foreigners, particularly those like me enjoying UN diplomatic privileges and facilities, had a very comfortable life in Teheran. What surprised me most, however, was the utter cynicism of those in high government positions. No one was serious about work and work in government offices moved at snail's pace. It was clear that the main objective of government service was to provide employment for some people. Most people in government service had incomes from side jobs or private business and the job in the government was considered only as an address of convenience. I found the work atmosphere quite frustrating and soon discovered that nobody at the higher levels of government was really concerned about what happened to the project. Although I had all the perquisites and material comforts of the high office I held, I felt unhappy at the fact that I was wasting my time in a sterile exercise of promoting small industries in which my Iranian counterparts had neither confidence nor commitment.

I was completing four years of service with the UN in Iran and another year of service would have made me eligible for a UN pension. At this stage, I received an enquiry from C.Subramaniam, Minister for Industries, Government of India, whether I would come back as Development Commissioner, Small Scale Industries, if offered the rank of Additional Secretary in the ministry and I readily accepted the offer. Ram Sathe, our Ambassador in Teheran at that time, told me when I informed him of my decision to return to India, that I was committing the biggest mistake of my life. His well-intentioned advice was that I should complete five years, earn my UN pension and leave only then. But I was more interested in job satisfaction than the UN pension and by the end of 1973 I returned to the job I had left ten years ago, but at the level of an Additional Secretary now.

I was in my new position hardly a year and a half when I received my promotion as Secretary. One day in June 1975 I was asked to see D.P. Chattopadhyaya, the Commerce Minister, whom I had never met before and I was told that it was in connection with my impending appointment as Secretary, Foreign Trade, in his ministry. There were a few officers senior to me still at Additional Secretary level and one of them was Additional Secretary in the Commerce ministry itself. I came to know later that the Prime Minister had approved my promotion as Secretary in the Commerce ministry overruling the point raised by the Cabinet Secretary that my appointment would cause embarrassment to the Additional Secretary already working there. The Additional Secretary got his promotion a few months later and was posted to another ministry.

When T.A. Pai, then Minister of Industries came to know of my impending promotion, he wanted to get the post of Development Commissioner upgraded to Secretary level in order to retain me in that post. I had to make a personal request to him to desist from such a move as I did not want to work in the same job again, even though it would be at a higher level. In June 1975, then, I was back in Udyog Bhavan as Secretary, Foreign Trade. I had worked in the same ministry as Under Secretary, Deputy Secretary and Joint Secretary and my new job was therefore, like homecoming for me.

Under the Janata government

1975-78 were eventful years in Indian history and in my life too. The Emergency, the general elections of 1977, the electoral defeat of Indira Gandhi, the establishment of the Janata government and the plethora of commissions of enquiry against Indira Gandhi and some of her colleagues brought in their wake many serious problems for civil servants. A big witch hunt began from the very day on which the new Janata government ministers were sworn in and heads started rolling with no time or opportunity given to any officer to explain. I remember the new minister Mohan Dharia, otherwise a man of great moral courage and principles, pulling out a small sheet of paper from his pocket within minutes of his sitting in the minister's chair in Udyog Bhavan after the swearing-in ceremony, reading out to me the names of certain officers working in my department and asking me to see that they proceeded on leave without any delay. Obviously the list had been prepared for the minister by others as he personally did not know any of the officers concerned, nor about the charges against them. They were suspects in the eyes of the new establishment for one reason or another and a decision had already been taken that their heads should roll even without waiting for any enquiry or explanation. This so called "cleaning up" operation was being done with great haste in almost all the ministries of the Government of India. This one act of the Janata government sent shock waves through the civil service and triggered off a demoralisation process which was to reach its nadir during the succeeding months of the Shah Commission and the host of other commissions of enquiry. Mohan Dharia treated me with unfailing courtesy and openly told everyone that he had great regard and respect for me particularly for keeping an unblemished record throughout the Emergency period, in spite of occupying a highly sensitive post. After a few months, I was designated as Commerce Secretary and the post of Secretary, Foreign Trade which I held till then was abolished.

What came as a great shock to me was that within days of the advent of the Janata government, the same characters who used to try and exert pressure in Udyog Bhavan for undeserved favours started making their rounds, now using the names and influence of the new power centres and influence brokers in the Janata establishment. Among various cases which I had to handle during my period as Commerce Secretary, I have to deal in some detail with one particular case as this finally brought me into direct confrontation with Prime Minister Morarji Desai and his powerful Principal Secretary, V. Shankar, and eventually resulted in my having to proceed on leave in 1978 and later opting for retirement from service.

The Janata government came to office with loud protests about the alleged malpractices of the Emergency days and declaration of their intention to usher in a clean administration. Some of us occupying key positions in the economic ministries soon found ourselves under pressure to stretch and bend rules to favour some individuals and business groups who were close to the new power centres. There were some such pressures during the previous government also, but I should say, at least from my own experience, that whenever I took a firm stand on what I considered to be correct, those who sought to apply pressures left me alone and never held my decisions against me. But my experience under the new government proved to be different and indeed bitter.

The import case of X

Now to the details of the case which brought me into trouble with the Janata government. In 1963, the government had introduced an export promotion scheme according to which exporters of certain non-traditional items could get import licence for certain high-premium items like drugs, pharmaceuticals, etc., up to 75% of the value of the export earnings. A particular group, which I shall call for purposes of this account, X, claimed that they had exported over £ 500,000 worth of zari goods to the UK and had become entitled to import licence up to 75% of the value. But the flaw in their case was that only a small part of the export earnings had been accounted for in India and they had already received their import entitlement for this. The bulk of the export earnings claimed by the firm as having accrued to their credit, had not been repatriated to India and therefore, there could be no corresponding entitlement for imports. Non-repatriation of foreign exchange earned through exports was a grave offence and the firm was guilty of this offence on their own admission. Further, the export incentive scheme itself had in the meantime been withdrawn by the government. The Enforcement Directorate had started proceedings against the firm for violation of foreign exchange regulations and had advised the ministry of Commerce against issue of any import licence in their favour. The firm, however, has been persistently trying for several years to get the benefit of imports.

In February 1977, just a few days before the General Elections, some people claiming to be very close to the Commerce Minister tried to bring pressure on me and my officers in the Import Control Wing to issue import licence to X, based on their old claim of exports. On 25 February 1977, a message was conveyed to me purporting to be from D.P. Chattopadhyaya, Commerce Minister, who was then on a long visit to Calcutta that he would like the file on X's case to be sent immediately to his Calcutta camp with my recommendation that final orders could be passed by the Commerce ministry without referring the case to the Finance ministry. Obviously, X were trying to get an order from the minister approving their claim for imports, short-circuiting the procedure for getting the views of the ministry of Finance. I sent the file to the minister that same day, but expressing my firm view that the case had to be referred to the ministry of Finance first. D.P. Chattopadhyaya, when he saw my advice on the file agreed with it and the efforts of the interested parties to get a licence issued in great haste were thus frustrated.

Pressure from PM's office

But my troubles on account of X's case were to start again within days of the establishment of the Janata government. X soon found powerful support in the circles close to the new Prime Minister and I came under strong pressure from V. Shankar, his Principal Secretary, for issue of the licence. I was surprised that the same group could apply their pressure tactics with the new government in such short time and with such ease.

V.Shankar sent for me and advised me to reconsider my stand on this case, dropping plain hints that he himself was under pressure to "do justice" in this case. Interferences from the Prime Minister's office those days were always on the ground that the Prime Minister wanted "justice" to be done and in all such cases the officers knew very well who the champions of "justice" were and why they were championing such cases.

I explained to Shankar the facts of the case, thinking that perhaps he did not know its full background. But he knew all the facts and was determined to twist my arms and try to make me agree to do what was patently irregular. He kept telephoning me frequently advising me about the importance of giving clearance to the licence and expressing annoyance at my insistence on rejecting the firm's claim as bogus. I wrote to Shankar on 8 May 1977 that since the Enforcement Directorate had advised that the party should repatriate the export proceeds first they should take up their claim with that directorate.

Shankar was not one who would give up merely on grounds of legal niceties and norms. He started applying pressure on the Director of Enforcement in the ministry of Finance to be "helpful" and this had the expected result. Most surprisingly, the Enforcement Directorate made a U-turn on its previous stand and sent a sort of clearance letter to the Commerce ministry leaving us to decide the case as we assessed its merits. I was indeed astonished that in a case involving huge amounts of foreign exchange, the Directorate of Enforcement could be so flexible and so easily reverse its earlier stand. But more surprise was in store for me. Shankar, one day, telephoned me to say that the Enforcement Directorate had withdrawn its objection and I was the only one now standing in the way of X getting a licence. When I replied that the Directorate had not given an unambiguous clearance, he handed over the phone to the Director of Enforcement who had already been summoned to his office and asked him to speak to me. The Director told me on Shankar's phone that the issue of the licence was now entirely a matter for the Commerce ministry to decide.

I was not prepared to be a party to a decision which in my judgement was dishonest and I decided to bring the whole case to the notice of the new Commerce minister, Mohan Dharia. In a note to him I explained the hollowness of the party's claim and personally briefed him about the pressures on me from the Prime Minister's office. Mohan Dharia fully supported my stand and assured me that he would stand by my decision. Shankar waited only for a few days to see whether I would relent.

In the meanwhile, rumours were afloat that I was being reverted to my parent cadre, Kerala. I was one of those civil servants who had been selected to the Central Administrative pool and the normal rules of reversion to the parent cadre did not apply in the case of pool officers. However, I was told that a decision had been taken by the Janata government to revert all those who had been with the Centre for more than ten years, irrespective of the fact whether they were members of the pool or not. When I checked about this with Nirmal Mukherjee, the Cabinet Secretary, he assured me that those who had less than two years to retire would not be reverted and since I fell under this category, I would certainly continue in the Central government's service. I knew that the rumours about my reversion were being deliberately floated by people as part of the pressure campaign to make me to yield to their request.

After exhausting all efforts at pressurising me, Shankar one day asked me to see him in his office and told me that the Prime Minister himself would be writing to Mohan Dharia about this case and that the Commerce ministry could, if they did not want to take a decision, refer the case to the Prime Minister's office for its advice. I did not at first believe that on a matter like this the Prime Minister would choose to intervene and I thought Shankar was mentioning the Prime Minister's name only as part of the pressure tactics. But a letter promptly arrived from the Prime Minister on 9 October 1977 saying that the case had been pending for over ten years and advising the minister that it may be finally disposed of in a fair and equitable manner. The letter was intended to show the importance attached to this case at the highest level. However, it should be said to the credit of Mohan Dharia that he stuck to the stand that it would be inadvisable to issue any licence to X when they had not accounted for the foreign exchange claimed to have been earned through their exports and when they were under investigation for this very offence.

I knew that Mohan Dharia's reply would only invite the wrath of the Prime Minister on me and I was now prepared for the worst.

There were one or two other cases of licences which had been brought to the personal notice of the Prime Minister as instances of my taking an "unhelpful" attitude. In fact, Mohan Dharia himself had told me that the Prime Minister had been making angry comments about me and asking why I was still continuing in the Central government. The Cabinet Secretary had also told me that the Prime Minister was very annoyed with me. I had explained to the Cabinet Secretary the full facts of the case and about the undue pressures being exerted by Shankar in getting a decision in favour of X. Now that the Prime Minister himself had intervened in the case, I knew that mine was an unequal fight and I would have to leave pretty soon. I decided that the facts should be recorded in the form of a note to the Cabinet Secretary before I was thrown out of my job. Accordingly, I sent him a detailed note on 17 November 1977 giving the full facts of the case and also an account of the various telephone calls and letters I had received from Shankar as part of his attempt to pressurise me to agree to the issue of licence. I requested the Cabinet Secretary to put up my note to the Prime Minister so that I would have the satisfaction of making my stand on this case known to the highest level in the government. The Cabinet Secretary assured me that my note would be put up to the Prime Minister but also warned me that I should be prepared for the consequences. I knew that I would be thrown out of the ministry, but I wanted to place the facts correctly in the form of a note so that there would be at least a record of the experiences I had to go through in trying to do what was correct and proper.

Nirmal Mukherjee later informed me about the Prime Minister's reaction on reading my note. He felt outraged that an officer could write so boldly about his office and insisted that I should be removed from my post that very day. Mukherjee told him that according to the decision already taken about pool officers, I should not be reverted to my home state at that stage as I had less than two years to retire. This made him very angry and he told the Cabinet Secretary that he was showing partiality to a fellow-Christian. This was a rather unfair remark for a person occupying the exalted position of the Prime Minister and Nirmal Mukherjee was quite upset. He told Morarji Desai that for the first time in his career he was being accused of communal bias and since the Prime Minister himself had done it, he considered it as an expression of lack of confidence in his objectivity and it would, therefore, not be appropriate for him to continue as Cabinet Secretary. Nirmal Mukherjee offered his resignation orally then and there and followed it up by a letter. Morarji Desai was not prepared for such a turn of events. He sent one of his trusted officers to Mukherjee to assure him of his continued confidence in him and to ask that he should withdraw his letter, which he did.

. I was at that time chairing a very important committee which was to recommend radical changes in import export policies and procedures. This committee, which later came to be known as the ''Alexander Committee'', had completed the major part of its work and had roused considerable interest and expectations among the business community. Nirmal Mukherjee informed the Prime Minister that if I were to leave at that stage, the committee's work would suffer badly and that it would be in government's own interest to allow me time to complete the report. Mohan Dharia also insisted that I should leave only after completing the work of the committee and it was finally agreed that I would stay on as Commerce Secretary till the report was ready.

I felt severely let down and mortified at the treatment that was being meted out to me for trying to be honest. Here was a government which had come to power professing to uphold the highest standards of integrity, punishing an officer because he refused to be a party to a dishonest deal. Mohan Dharia fully sympathised with me in my predicament but told me plainly that he was helpless in this matter. The immediate thought that occurred to me was that I should quit without bothering as to what happened to the committee's work. I argued with myself that I had no need to slave for a few weeks more to complete the work I had taken, after the way the government had treated me. But my own sense of duty finally prevailed and I completed the work of the committee by the end of January 1978. I presented the report to the minister on 31 January and the next day proceeded on leave.

I was very clear in my mind that I would not join service in my parent cadre in Kerala. I was the senior most officer of the Kerala cadre of the IAS at that time. On an earlier occasion when the Kerala Chief Minister, Achutha Menon, had asked for my services for appointment as Chief Secretary, Indira Gandhi had not agreed to it on the ground that I was then holding a very important assignment at the Centre. Now I was to go back to the Kerala government as I was being unceremoniously thrown out of the

Central government. I thought it would be humiliating to go back to the state in such circumstances and I decided to look for an opportunity of going for a short spell of UN service from where I could send in my letter of retirement from the IAS with honour and dignity. I had come away from UN service twice before to work for my own government and I was now being compelled to go back to the UN to preserve my self-respect.

The persecution continues

Morarji Desai's dislike for me did not end with sending me out of the Commerce ministry. I was too small a person in rank and status compared with the Prime Minister of India and he should not normally have cared to know what I did after I left the Central government. But this was not to be the case with Morarji Desai.

The post of Secretary General of the International Sugar Organisation, London, had fallen vacant and my name had been sponsored for this assignment by the Government of India as I had the requisite qualifications and background. This was done in the routine course by the Cabinet Secretary after obtaining the approval of Charan Singh, who was then the minister for Home Affairs in the Janata government. The selection to this post was to be done by a board representing member countries of the organisation. The ministry of External Affairs had been informed by our High Commissioner in London that I stood a reasonable chance of being selected if India could, in turn, support some other countries which had fielded candidates for other positions in the organisation. It is the normal practice in selections to positions in international organisations to try and enlist support for one post in exchange for support for other positions in which other countries are interested. As soon as the ministry of External Affairs came to know that the prospects of my getting the top post were fair, they took the usual step of sending out telegrams to our Ambassadors in the concerned countries asking them to enlist support for me and in exchange offer support for candidates from some of these countries for the other posts. Copies of these telegrams were sent to the Prime Minister for routine information, but when Morarji Desai saw these telegrams he was very angry to find that the government was extending support to me.

He sent for the Cabinet Secretary and took strong objection to my name having been sponsored without his approval and wanted it immediately withdrawn. Nirmal Mukherjee pointed out that the Home Minister who was the competent authority had approved the sponsoring and it would not be proper to withdraw my name at that stage. By then Morarji Desai had begun to have his own troubles with his Home Minister and he did not want to create a new problem by overruling Charan Singh's decision in this matter. He, therefore, instructed the Cabinet Secretary that no effort be made at canvassing support for my candidature by the ministry of External Affairs and the Cabinet Secretary like a disciplined civil servant conveyed these instructions to Vishnu Ahuja, Secretary in the ministry of External Affairs, who was dealing with the case.

In the meantime, the Government of India was getting enquiries from other countries about our support for one post or the other in exchange for their support for my candidature but Vishnu Ahuja did not take any action on these enquiries. When I found that the ministry of External Affairs was not replying promptly to the enquiries, I asked Ahuja about it. He told me, with evident unhappiness, that he had been instructed by higher quarters not to do anything more about my candidature. I immediately sought a meeting with Nirmal Mukherjee who told me frankly how the Prime Minister had forbidden any support for my candidature for this post. I listened to him calmly and without any bitterness. However, I asked him whether it was the Prime Minister's stand that he would rather have a non-Indian for this post than see me getting it. Of course, I did not expect a reply to this. I told Mukherjee that I fully understood his position in this case and would not in any way embarrass him by asking any help from the government thereafter in this matter. Mukherjee felt very unhappy because he knew that this was a highly unfair action, and one which I did not deserve. I went through the motion of appearing before the Selection Board in London as my name was already on the panel but as anticipated, I did not get the job as I did not have the support of my own government.

However, my efforts at getting an international assignment were not to be frustrated merely because I had incurred the displeasure of such a powerful person like the Prime Minister of India. After I returned to the Government of India service from my last UN assignment, I had off and on been receiving enquiries about my interest in and availability for further assignment with the UN. Thus far I had not shown any interest in such offers. Now having made up my mind that I would rather opt for retirement than accept a reversion to the Kerala cadre, I decided to take a short UN assignment and to send in my letter of retirement from there.

I did not have to wait for long. The International Trade Center, UNCTAD, GATT at Geneva offered me an assignment as Senior Adviser to the head of the organisation and I promptly accepted it. I was thus back in UN service for the third time in my career in June 1978.

My third UN assignment

I have already said that I had left the UN service in Iran without completing five years to become entitled to a UN pension. As soon as I joined ITC, I was told of the most welcome decision the UN had taken that those with previous UN service could revalidate such service for purposes of pension on taking new assignments, by paying the pension contribution for the period. In my case, I could claim the previous four years of service in Iran if I could serve for one year in ITC for purposes of eligibility for pension. In the normal course I would never have gone for any more UN service at that stage of my career. Now, when I found that I could revalidate my previous service and earn a handsome UN pension, the first thought that occurred to me was how Morarji Desai had become a real benefactor of mine. I promptly sent in my letter of retirement from government service and accepted a year's contract as Senior Adviser to the Director of ITC.

Very soon I was to have more unexpected luck. Within a year of my joining as Senior Adviser, the post of executive head of ITC became vacant and the authorities of the UN and the GATT which control ITC decided to select me as head of the organisation. They also decided to recommend the upgradation of the post of the head of the organisation to the level of Assistant Secretary General. This proposal was approved by the Fifth Committee of the UN General Assembly, even though it had been strongly opposed by the UN Budget Committee particularly by all the influential members of the Budget Committee such as the U.S.A. and the U.K. By this time, the political convulsions in India had swept Morarji Desai off his Prime Ministership and there was no risk of the Government of India not supporting the case for upgradation of my post in the UN Assembly. Charan Singh was the new Prime Minister and his Commerce minister Hitendra Desai had issued instructions to the

Indian Mission in New York to canvass support for the proposal for upgradation of the post. The post was eventually upgraded and I was given the rank of Assistant Secretary General. With Morarji Desai in power this would not have happened.

I found my job as Executive Director extremely interesting, as I had the freedom to introduce several new programmes in the technical services activities of the ITC. Unlike my two previous UN assignments, I derived great job satisfaction from this assignment and received full support from the main donor countries and Advisory Committee of the ITC in the new projects I had started for trade promotion in developing countries in Africa, Latin America and Asia. A new office building for ITC was being constructed at a central place in Geneva and ITC was well on its way to acquiring a new identity and personality of its own and I was enjoying my new work thoroughly.

Offer of post from Indira Gandhi

In the meanwhile, the political scene in India was changing fast, leading to unexpected changes in my life too. The Janata leaders who had come to power professing lofty principles and high ideals, soon got busy with personal rivalries and quarrels and were seen to be more interested in pulling each other down than running the government. The stink of corruption, the countless commissions of enquiry and witch-hunt had brought the whole government into disrepute and people began to talk nostalgically about the virtues of Indira Gandhi's effective and efficient government. Indira Gandhi's victory at Chickmagalur towards the end of 1978 gave hope to millions of ordinary people of India who were yearning for a change.

I was one of those millions who sincerely believed that only a dynamic leader like Indira Gandhi could save the country at that stage. I had always been an ardent admirer of Indira Gandhi as a political leader and had believed that she alone, among the Congress leaders then, could carry forward the message of secularism and modernism which had been the legacy of Jawaharlal Nehru to the nation.

From my student days Nehru had been my hero and I had felt proud to belong to Nehru's India. As a young man I had vowed that when I got married and if I had a son I would name him ''Jawahar'' and behold I could fulfil this dream when my first son was born in

1949. My son, when he grew up was not as excited as I was about his name and perhaps in this he was typical of the new generation in India which refused to be hero-worshippers. When he was selected to the IAS in 1971 and was assigned to the Kerala cadre, he found his name Jawahar rather strange in the circles in which he had to move in the South. As a young man who went to school and college in Delhi, the name did not appear to be strange, but in Kerala this was very new name. He, therefore, conveniently abbreviated his name Jawahar Cherian Alexander into a simple J.C. Alexander. But at home and among our friends and relations he is still Jawahar – a proud reminder to me of my profound respect for that great man of character and integrity.

Indira Gandhi, daughter of Jawaharlal Nehru, was thus a ready-made heroine for me and I was mentally always on her side in all her fights with her political adversaries. But being a civil servant, I could not give expression to my loyalty or support to any political leader and I continued to remain a distant and silent admirer all these years. When the results of her Chickmagalur elections reached me in Geneva, I was no longer in government service and I sent her a letter of good wishes and congratulations, least expecting a reply. But I received the following warm and affectionate reply from her:

P/7665   12, Willingdon Crescent,
New Delhi.

10th December, 1978

Dear Mr. Alexander,

Thank you for your letter of the 8th November. It is good of you to write.

I have heard of the circumstances in which you opted for retirement. I felt it was a pity since the Government is in dire need of honest and competent people like you. However your new job is an interesting one as well as important. I am sure you will do well there.

With all good wishes to you and your wife for Christmas and the New Year.

Yours sincerely,

Sd/- (INDIRA GANDHI)

Mr. P.C. Alexander,
Apt. 1751, 17 ave. de Bude,
1202 Geneva, Switzerland.

The next time I wrote to her was when she was returned to power with a massive majority in January 1980. Indians living abroad had been following with great disgust the manoeuvrings and manipulations for power by politicians who preached high principles but seldom practised them and the splits, defections and horse-trading which were going on among them in their relentless chase of ministerial chairs. The news of Indira Gandhi's triumphant return created in us a sense of pride in our country's democratic system. I wrote to her on 10 January 1980, congratulating her on her election victory. Her reply of 13 February, just a month after taking over as Prime Minister, shows her deep worries about the situation of law and order and the economy she had inherited:

New Delhi
February 13, 1980

Dear Mr. Alexander,

Thank you for your letter of congratulations. I appreciate your writing.

The situation is very serious especially the law and order and the economy. Both are linked. Our Government doesn't know where to begin to sort things out especially as the opposition is out to obstruct and disrupt in every possible way.

Yours sincerely,

Sd/- (INDIRA GANDHI)
Prime Minister

Mr. P.C. Alexander
Apt. 1244, 12 ave. de Bude
1202 Geneva
Switzerland

Indira Gandhi had asked Krishnaswamy Rao Sahib, who was Secretary to the outgoing Prime Minister Charan Singh, to continue as Secretary to Prime Minister. She had made it known to him that she was on the lookout for a new Secretary and he was to stay on in this post only as an interim assignment. As weeks went by, Rao Sahib proved to be both trustworthy and efficient and her relations with him were smooth and relaxed. Still, the search was on for a new Secretary.

I came to know by the middle of 1980 that I was the top name in her list of probable choices for this post. As I have said earlier, my contacts with her were very limited and except for the brief exchange of letters, I was somewhat of a stranger to her. She herself was not sure whether I would be willing to leave my senior UN position in Geneva for a Secretary's job in Delhi. Shiv Shankar, the Law Minister in her Cabinet and one of the ministers close to her, was visiting Geneva to attend a UN conference there and she had asked him to meet me and discreetly check on my willingness and availability for the job without directly making an offer on her behalf. This was the first time I was meeting Shiv Shankar. His informal manner and intense loyalty to Indira Gandhi impressed me. He told me that he had asked to see me as Indira Gandhi had spoken to him about her high regard for me and had specially wanted that he should meet me. We both avoided talking about my taking up any position in the government. Shiv Shankar realised that if I left the UN job it would be a loss to India as another Indian was not likely to be selected for this post, but he conveyed the message to me in his own diplomatic way that Indira Gandhi would be very pleased if I decided to return to the service of the Government of India.

By about October 1980, I received a message through an officer visiting Geneva that she would like to meet me on my next visit to Delhi. He informed me that I was still the first name on her list for consideration for the post of Secretary to the Prime Minister and that she would consider other names only if I were not available. I thought I should meet her in Delhi, since she had been so keen to ascertain my interest in this matter. I had planned to visit Delhi during November-December on home leave and I wrote to Indira Gandhi's office seeking an appointment with her.

While I felt honoured to know that I was being considered for such a position of trust by Indira Gandhi, I did not feel very enthusiastic about the proposal at first, as I was not sure whether I would be able to function effectively in the Delhi set-up as it was then. I was aware of the various groups and cliques operating in the corridors of power in Delhi and I also knew that some of these groups greatly resented the idea of my coming into a post close to the Prime Minister. They knew that I would not allow myself to be manipulated or controlled by them and were therefore, trying to thwart my prospects coming into this position. I feel uncomfortable in an atmosphere of intrigues and group politics and had strong reservations about working in such an environment.

The question which worried me most was whether after leaving a challenging and highly satisfying UN assignment, I would be effective in the new environment. To me, the privilege of serving Indira Gandhi as her Secretary was more than adequate compensation for leaving my UN job. But the thought that I might be jumping into an arena where I might find myself ineffective continued to gnaw at me and I felt unable to make up my mind on this score. Obviously, it was improper to express my doubts to the Prime Minister or even to discuss such matters with her. I had seen some reports in Indian journals later saying that I had asked for an assurance from Indira Gandhi that I would have a free hand in my work and would not allow any interference. Indira Gandhi was not one to whom conditions could be stipulated, or from whom prior assurances could be asked for, and I was not going to talk like this with her. My respect for her was far too great for any such talk. It was entirely up to me to decide whether I would be able to work effectively in the conditions prevailing in Delhi at that time and I thought I should take a little more time to make my own assessment on this aspect. Therefore, I went to her office in South Block one day in November 1980 for meeting her, with no intention of either committing myself or of asking for any assurances from her.

I found Indira Gandhi in a very relaxed mood. She enquired about the functioning of ITC which I was heading at that time and to what extent my Indian experience in the area of trade promotion was proving useful in my present position. After about fifteen minutes of general talk on the UN and its various activities and life in Geneva, she came to the point. She said that she was finding it difficult to get the right men for certain crucial positions. "We have many experienced and competent men in our country," she said, "but when it comes to choosing the right persons for certain key positions, I find I have a problem. Take for example, the position of Secretary to the Prime Minister. I have not yet been able to make a proper choice and that is why I wanted to meet you and discuss the possibility of your coming on to this post". I knew that she expected me to say then and there that I was quite willing to accept this post. But my fears still haunted me and I thought I should take a little more time to gauge the working environment in Delhi before taking the final plunge. I told her that I was on my way to Manila to spend three weeks with my son who was working in the Asian Development Bank there and that I would meet her again on my way back from Manila.

I discussed this matter with some of my close friends and well-wishers in Delhi. I found that some cliques which were dominant in the Emergency days had become active after the elections and there was very little change in their style and methods of operation. At the same time, I was told by friends who knew Indira Gandhi closely that she, herself, wanted to make radical changes in the Government's style of working and to clip the wings of some persons who were misusing the power and influence they enjoyed because of their close association with her. In fact, I was told that the main reason for her preferring me was the confidence she had that I would be able to bring in some degree of freshness, discipline and objectivity in the decision-making process in the Prime Minister's office and restore confidence in the fairness of such processes.

On my return to Delhi from Manila by mid-December 1980, I found that Indira Gandhi had taken my meeting with her as willingness on my part to take up the post and all that remained was to settle the details such as the date of joining, terms of appointment, etc. I was in Delhi only for two days and I was asked to meet a senior cabinet colleague of the Prime Minister to talk over these matters. I met this minister at his office only for a few minutes and told him that I was proceeding to Kerala for a week and would come back to Delhi to see Indira Gandhi again before leaving for Geneva. He said he would fix a date and time for my meeting and let me know by telegram about this at my Kerala address.

What followed was an unexpected confusion, deliberately created by some interested parties, according to some of my knowledgeable friends, to prevent my coming to this job. I did not receive any telegram from the minister and I returned to Geneva without coming to Delhi for a meeting with the Prime Minister. Indira Gandhi, a few weeks later it appears, expressed surprise that I did not meet her before leaving India and asked the minister why he had not arranged the meeting. It was only then that the minister contacted me on the phone at Geneva and asked why I did not come to Delhi to see the Prime Minister in spite of his sending a telegram to me. I told him I never received any such telegram and he should check with his own office as to what happened to the telegram if he had authorised one. Pupul Jayakar, who had always been strongly urging me to come back to India telephoned to say that Indira Gandhi was intrigued by the fiasco of the telegram and that I should straightaway inform the Prime Minister of my willingness to accept the job if I had made up my mind. Almost immediately after Pupul Jayakar's message, Krishnaswamy Rao Sahib, Secretary to the Prime Minister spoke to me on the phone and told me that the Prime Minister had asked him to ascertain from me the terms I would like to have for my appointment. I told Rao Sahib to inform Indira Gandhi that I never received any message asking me to come again to Delhi, but that I had decided to accept the appointment. I said that I had nothing to say about the period of the contract or the emoluments of the job and whatever she decided would be acceptable to me. I received confirmation the next day that my rank would be that of Principal Secretary and that I would have a tenure without any period being fixed in advance but which could be terminated on three months notice on either side.

I gave notice to the UN authorities about my intention to resign my appointment as Executive Director of ITC with effect from 1 May 1981 and returned to Government of India service exactly three years after leaving it.

I had left government service in 1978 with no thought of ever returning to it. Strange indeed are the quirks of fate.

2

INDIRA GANDHI'S PERSONALITY AND STYLE OF WORKING

Briefing me about my job

I took over as Principal Secretary to Prime Minister on Saturday, 2 May 1981. Krishnaswamy Rao Sahib had taken charge as Cabinet Secretary the previous day. We met the Prime Minister together for a few minutes on the 2nd forenoon and this was my formal reporting to duty. There was very little time then to talk on official matters. Indira Gandhi was to leave on an official visit to Switzerland, Kuwait, and U.A.E. on the 5th of May and I was to accompany her on those visits.

The opportunity of accompanying the Prime Minister on her visit abroad within three days of taking over as Principal Secretary proved to be a very good introduction to my new responsibilities. I could spend about eight days travelling with her in different countries, watching her in different situations – discussing with heads of international agencies, heads of governments, attending official banquets, meeting Indians living in these countries, holding press conferences and TV interviews – and thus get initiated into my new job quicker than would have been the case in Delhi. During these travels, I had the opportunity to study her style and method of work very closely and this turned out to be a very valuable experience.

Travel abroad with Indira Gandhi was always in good comfort; Air-India spared no efforts to make her and those accompanying her comfortable. But my first travel with Indira Gandhi was not exactly a comfortable one. A few days before the Prime Minister was to begin her journey, 'Makalu' , the Air-India plane which was to carry her was found to have been tampered with. Sabotage was suspected, causing last-minute cancellation of the plans to travel by Air-India carriers and a switch to a smaller Indian Airlines plane which did not have the facilities for a long air journey by a VIP. A small cabin was improvised for use by the Prime Minister and it lacked even the elementary comforts required for a long-distance journey. The plane had to halt at Muscat and Cyprus for refuelling before reaching Geneva.

My first briefing on my new job was in the Prime Minister's cabin in the Indian Airlines plane. Within an hour of our take-off from Delhi, Indira Gandhi called me to her cabin and said that she wanted to tell me a few things about her government's policies and work programmes, so that I could know what her principal concerns were. For well over an hour, she explained to me the main problems facing her government and what she considered to be the priority tasks for her administration. They were, she explained, restoring the health of the economy, improving the efficiency of the administrative machinery and arresting the deterioration in the law and order situation. The Akali agitation had not yet taken the violent turn it did in a few months time, but she had sensed the potential of trouble in Punjab and was deeply worried about it.

She explained to me in great detail the weaknesses in her own party and how the party organisation was proving to be ineffective in providing support to the government in implementing the promises in the election manifesto. She told me that she would be spending a lot of time rebuilding the party from the shambles it had been in for the last few years and this was a major task by itself. She said that there was need to infuse a new life into administration as she found that the administrative machinery had practically ground to a halt during the Janata regime.

The talk then turned to her own family and she gave a candid assessment of the personalities of her two sons. She explained how Sanjay had come to play the important role he did in the party and how he was helpful in preserving the morale of the Congress party faithfuls during the difficult days of the Janata period. I took special note of the detached manner in which she spoke of Sanjay's death as if it were just another event in Indian history unconnected with her personal life. I was astonished to see how well she had got reconciled to the great personal tragedy that had occurred in her life only a few months ago. She spoke with great warmth and appreciation about the manner in which Rajiv had come forward to take over some of her responsibilities relating to party work.

Finally, she told me that it was her desire that I should take interest in every aspect of the work she had to handle and that I should not consider my work limited to administration or economic matters.

It was a thorough briefing on my new role and I was particularly surprised by the candour with which she spoke to me about her own family. Perhaps, this was her way of indicating to me that she was going to involve me in all areas of concern to her and not merely in matters of administration.

I shall now attempt to present a picture of Indira Gandhi's personality and style of working. It is difficult to make a proper assessment of a highly complex personality like Indira Gandhi; I can only try to give the impressions I have gained of her and her style of work, judging from the different situations in which I have seen her operating. Taken together, these, I hope will give an insight into her personality and outlook on life.

Versatile interests and tastes

What impressed me most about Indira Gandhi was the versatility of her interests and tastes. The public at large knew her as the Prime Minister and the undisputed leader of the Congress party. To most people, she was a political leader and the coverage in the press in India and abroad was invariably about her pronouncements and activities as a politician. But those who knew her closely knew that she was equally interested and active in a wide range of subjects which had little to do with politics. Her interest in flowers and trees, forests and wild life, mountains and environment and arts and architecture was as intense as her interest in politics.

Other equally intense interests for her were the amelioration of the sufferings of the physically handicapped, particularly the blind, and the eradication of leprosy. The cause of children and women and the welfare of the tribal communities was another area of great concern for her. Indira Gandhi's interest in and commitment for these causes were not just peripheral, but total. I have often wondered how a person so deeply involved in politics and administration could have such intense involvement and interest in these matters. In fact, even in the midst of the busiest of schedules, she would always find time for meeting persons connected with these causes and even give precedence to such meetings over other official engagements.

The "Iron Lady" image

The "Iron Lady" image which the media in India and abroad had built up around Indira Gandhi is a totally ill-fitting and undeserving one. Perhaps this image stuck to her after the Bangladesh war. No doubt she had strong convictions of her own on many matters and would not hesitate to take such action as she considered appropriate, without bothering about the criticisms it might provoke. But this was only one aspect of her personality. By nature, she was neither hard-hearted nor dictatorial as is often made out by her critics. The decision to go to war with Pakistan was forced on her by the stupidity of General Yahya Khan in ordering the strike on Indian air-fields without any provocation. Yahya underestimated the grit and courage of Indira Gandhi and Pakistan had to pay a heavy price for this. While the war was forced on her, her decision to announce a unilateral ceasefire and to recognise Bangladesh as a new sovereign country was entirely hers. It is in these two decisions that the remarkable qualities of courage and statesmanship of Indira Gandhi come out most conspicuously. She had told me how almost her entire cabinet and the Chiefs of the Armed Forces had vehemently opposed the idea of a ceasefire when India could, if it wanted, wrest large chunks of territory on the Western front immediately after Pakistan's humiliating surrender at Dacca. But Indira Gandhi's statesmanship prevailed over the quite understandable wishes of her political colleagues and military advisers and a ceasefire was declared without going in for territorial gains.

Recognition of Bangladesh as a sovereign State at that juncture prevented the possibility of that country emerging as an autonomous unit in a loose Pakistani confederation. If Indira Gandhi had not taken the crucial decision to accord full-scale recognition to Bangladesh, the history of the subcontinent could have taken a different course. International pressure would have become irresistible to find some sort of a face-saving formula in order to keep, at least nominally, the territorial integrity of Pakistan. If time was allowed for an examination of the pros and cons of an independent Bangladesh and a Bangladesh as an autonomous unit of the Pakistani confederation, the decision would in all probability have been in favour of the latter. It was here that Indira Gandhi showed exceptional courage and foresight. India's promptness in recognising Bangladesh took the issue out of the hands of constitutional pundits and international pressure groups. After India's announcement of its decision to recognise Bangladesh, it was only a question of a few days for the new nation to gain worldwide recognition. Indira Gandhi's decision in announcing a unilateral ceasefire and prompt recognition of Bangladesh as an independent nation demonstrated the cool courage of a great statesman and not the brashness of an "Iron Lady".

Perhaps, another reason for her "Iron Lady" image was her alleged role in dismissing the first communist government of E.M.S. Namboodiripad in Kerala in 1957. Indian communists have been persistently propagating the story that it was Indira Gandhi who as Congress President prevailed upon her father to dismiss the ministry in the wake of the mass agitation known as "Vimochana Samaram" or "war of liberation". In fact, even several Congressmen hold on to this story as authentic and sometimes cite it as an example of Indira Gandhi's courage in decision-making. The Indian communists, have of course, described this as the most unpardonable crime against democracy and have not grown tired of repeating this charge against her on every possible occasion. But the fact is that it was not Indira Gandhi who played the crucial role in the dismissal of the communist government but Pandit Pant, then Home Minister. Indira Gandhi told me on a number of occasions when this subject came up for discussion between us that it was Pant's insistence on dismissing the communist ministry that really prevailed with Prime Minister Nehru. I once asked her why she had not refuted this allegation against her even though the communist parties had been using this as an example of her high-handedness and anti-democratic attitude. Her reply was typical of her attitude to the criticism of opposition parties against her. "If I am to refute all the allegations against me by the opposition parties", she told me, "I will have no time for anything else".

Indira Gandhi has been most unfairly criticised by some people for her alleged involvement in the dismissal of N.T. Rama Rao's government in August 1984. The truth is that she came to know of Governor Ramlal's action, for the first time, when I got the news from the Intelligence Bureau and brought it to her notice. She was quite upset and annoyed at the action taken and even took it as part of a move on the part of some interested groups close to her to malign her and weaken her authority. M.G. Ramachandran, Chief Minister of Tamil Nadu, telephoned me from Madras early in the morning of 21st August 1984 strongly suggesting that she should repudiate this allegation publicly as the people in the South were beginning to question her bona fides in this sordid affair. I conveyed this to her and she readily agreed to do so and emphatically repudiated the charge during her intervention in the debate on the Andhra Pradesh developments later in the day in the Parliament. Nevertheless, some critics keep on repeating this allegation against her.

Even though she publicly refuted the charge about her involvement in the dismissal of the N.T. Rama Rao ministry, she chose not to do so about the charge relating to the dismissal of the communist government in Kerala, mainly because she did not want to be seen as shifting the responsibility to Pandit Pant who was not alive and for whom she had great personal respect and regard. She had, on several occasions, mentioned to me the communists' allegations against her in this matter as an example of the opposition parties' campaign of vilification against her, based on their own assumptions.

Indira Gandhi always remained basically an Indian woman. She was feminine not only in her personal grace and charm, but in her attitudes, reflexes and reactions. She was not a feminist in the usual sense of the term; in fact, she disliked many things associated with modern feminist movements. She sincerely believed that given the opportunity, women could do as well as men in any field. What they lacked in most societies was the opportunity to equip themselves and when equipped, the opportunity to prove their worth. She was acutely conscious of the many disabilities which women had to suffer in Indian society. She did not believe that men alone were responsible for the sad plight of Indian women. She used to say that women themselves were often responsible for aggravating the miseries of fellow women.

A journalist once described Indira Gandhi, in what was intended to be high praise to her, as the "only man in her cabinet" and this has often been quoted in complimentary tributes to her. Indira Gandhi heartily disliked the sexist slant in this tribute. She once told me that statements like this revealed the arrogance in the thinking of some men that courage and excellence are the monopoly of men. If a woman showed such qualities, she had to be described as a man and if a man displayed lack of such qualities he had to be described as a woman. She strongly resented the condescending superiority complex underlying such statements. She told me that the worst example of the sexist superiority complex in India was the practice of making mock presents of glass bangles to political leaders as a gesture of insult. If a political leader showed weakness or cowardice in a crisis, the ultimate insult was to present him with bangles, which in other words was calling him a woman. She felt sad that this type of sexist slur was commonly accepted even by persons who were otherwise not biased against women. She mentioned this as an example to show how deep-rooted the prejudices against women in India are.

Neatness and orderliness

Indira Gandhi attached great importance to neatness and orderliness in everything she did and in the environment in which she lived or worked. A flowerpot in the wrong place, a chair in an awkward position, a photograph hanging slanted on the wall, pencils, pens and stationery carelessly thrown about on the table or dust or dirt in a corner would immediately attract her attention. Often she would not wait for an orderly or someone else to do the job of restoring neatness and order in her office; she would do such jobs herself shaming others who should have been more conscientious in their work.

Once as I entered her office in the Parliament House for my usual morning meeting with her, I did not find her on her chair. Looking around, I saw her washing the lower parts of the leaves of the plants in the flowerpots in her room with a wet towel. I was somewhat amused at the sight of the Prime Minister of India with a towel and a jug of water in her hands, diligently going ahead with the work of cleaning the leaves. It took a few minutes for her to complete the work of the cleaning she had started but she asked me not to wait till she had finished this gardener's work and I carried on my discussions on high matters of State with the Prime Minister while she was cleaning each leaf of the plant with great care and dexterity.

Good hostess

For the banquets and receptions hosted by Indira Gandhi, she herself decided the menu and often the seating arrangement at the table. Sometimes, protocol had to be overlooked because she wanted to place near the visiting dignitaries persons who could carry on a useful conversation. Some Indians, including some of the senior cabinet ministers invited to her banquets, had the habit of carrying on conversation with only their Indian colleagues, sometimes even across the table, ignoring the presence of foreign guests sitting next to them. Some Indian dignitaries would remain silent throughout the banquet without even attempting to start a conversation with the guests next to them. Indira Gandhi used to note these things carefully and did not hesitate to tell the persons concerned about the importance of using such opportunities for exchange of views and establishing personal contacts. She herself was an enchanting conversationalist on these occasions. She would relate interesting anecdotes, always appropriate for the occasion, and make her guests feel at ease. At the same time, she would be keeping a vigilant watch on the service at the table and would pull up the persons concerned if she found service sloppy or careless.

While eating, she would sometimes explain to the interested guests how a particular dish had been prepared or in which part of India a particular delicacy was popular. Though a frugal eater, she took great delight in ensuring that her guests enjoyed their meals. She had no serious taboos except that she did not take beef or alcoholic drinks. While toasting or replying to toasts she would raise a glass of fruit juice which would invariably be placed before her. If she found no glass of juice in a banquet, as had happened sometimes in banquets hosted by dignitaries in foreign countries, she would quietly raise the glass of wine up to the lips without tasting it or insisting on getting a glass of juice for the occasion. She had no objection to the Indians accompanying her taking alcoholic drinks on such occasions, but she strongly disliked excessive drinking on their part and had generally a contempt for persons known to be addicted to drinks. Sometimes, while discussing important appointments, she would tell me why she considered a particular person unsuitable because of the reports she had about his excessive drinking habits. She could not stand hot food or spicy pickles. But being a generous hostess, she always remembered that I liked pickles and would especially instruct the waiter to place a bottle of pickles or hot sauce in front of me whenever I attended dinners hosted by her. She believed that most South Indians liked hot food and would specially arrange for hot pickles and sauce for P.V. Narasimha Rao and R.Venkataraman, if they were at a dinner with her.

While travelling abroad, she was always mindful of the special requirements of some of the members of her entourage. Sharada Prasad, Prime Minister's Information Adviser, is an incorrigible but never-complaining vegetarian. Once visiting a Gulf country, she noticed at a banquet that almost every item served was non-vegetarian. She turned to me seated near her at the high table and asked in Hindi whether "poor Sharada was getting anything to eat". I could see from my seat that Sharada Prasad was not exactly starving. He could always have a hearty meal if some rice and curds were around and I assured Indira Gandhi that Sharada was doing perfectly well. This was not just a casual enquiry about one member of her delegation. She was genuinely interested in the comforts of those travelling with her and the feminine instinct in her made her ask such questions about the welfare of others.

Working methods and style

Indira Gandhi had not set aside any fixed hours for her office work. Whenever she was in Delhi, she would come to her office in the South Block between 10 and 10.30 in the morning and go home for lunch normally between 1.30 and 2.00 p.m.. Again she would be back in the office between 3.00 and 3.30 p.m. and be there till 7.00 or 8.00 p.m. and on some days till even 9.00, depending on the pressure of work. During Parliament sessions, her own office would be shifted from the South Block to the Parliament House. Her personal staff would move with her to the Parliament House while I and other officers of her Secretariat would continue to work from the South Block. Meetings of the Cabinet and Cabinet Committees during Parliament sessions were held after 6.00 p.m. and on such days she would go home only well after 9.00 p.m. If there was some important development requiring urgent consideration, she would call members of the Cabinet Committee on Political Affairs and the Cabinet Secretary and me for meetings at very short notice at the residence at any time of the night.

She would speak to me on telephone at my residence on urgent matters, whatever be the time of the night and sometimes ask me to go over to her house for discussions at even late hours of the night. If I had to be called to the house on a Sunday morning, she would invariably ask her P.A. to check first whether I was planning to go to Church for the service. I was not very regular in Church attendance, but she took special care to see that demands on my time on a Sunday morning did not in any way interfere with my attending the Church service, if I wished to do so.

On any working day, the first engagement of the Prime Minister after reaching office was to meet me. I would take with me the papers which required discussion and obtain her orders on them. She herself would always have a few papers to be handed over to me. My discussions would cover a wide range of subjects, such as important appointments, sensitive political and defence matters, law and order problems, issues coming up for discussion in the Parliament or before a Cabinet meeting, major foreign policy problems which required attention by the Prime Minister and important letters and notes received from her cabinet colleagues. During the years of the Punjab agitation, this subject figured in my talks with the Prime Minister almost every day, often two or three times a day. I used to keep her informed of every important development relating to the Punjab and appraise her of the recommendations of the Secretaries' Committee dealing with Punjab and the related security problems. She would always give clear and precise instructions on every issue placed before her. Sometimes, she would suggest that the matter might be placed before the Cabinet Committee on Political Affairs. On some very important issues, she would have informal consultations with a few selected Cabinet colleagues individually before arriving at a decision.

She had given me the privilege of expressing my views freely even on matters on which she held totally different views. Sometimes, I used to have arguments with her to emphasise some aspects which I felt were being overlooked by her or to warn her about what I thought would be the consequences of a particular line of action she proposed to take. In the early days of my working with her, I used to be very apologetic in coming out so openly and directly on a particular issue and I used to preface my views with some words of regret. "I am sorry, Madam, my views on this are different and I feel I should state them before you'', I would start with some such introduction. She allowed me full freedom to say what I felt on a subject and would talk to me with equal frankness if she felt that what I proposed was unacceptable for any reason – often some important political consideration which had to be taken into account by her. Even in matters where she disagreed with my views totally, she would allow me freedom to state all the arguments in their support. She had trust in my motives and was genuinely appreciative of the frankness with which I presented my views. Later, whenever I started my usual introduction, "I am sorry, Madam, but I have to state my views", she would cut me short with an affectionate smile and say "You don't have to be sorry. I want you to say all that you want to say". After a few times of my being told "I want you to say all that you want to say", I stopped prefacing my statements with polite apologies and always came out directly with whatever I wanted to say on any issue. It is not that she was willing to accept my views always. Sometimes she did not; sometimes she accepted part of my suggestions. But she always listened to what I had to say and made me feel that she attached importance to my views on these matters.

In most cases, after discussions with Indira Gandhi, I would record the decisions on the file and communicate them to the minister or officer concerned without troubling her again for written orders on the file. In specially sensitive cases, I would record the decisions and submit the note to her to enable her to make any changes in the formulation of decisions, if she chose to do so. In some cases, the Prime Minister's instructions would be conveyed over the telephone to the persons concerned. There was a great deal of trust involved in this system of working.

Here, I should make a special mention of the fact that I had always the most cordial relations with Cabinet Secretary Krishnanswamy Rao Sahib. We had implicit trust in each other's integrity. Sometimes, if the Cabinet Secretary and I had a difference of views on a particular issue, he would leave it to me to present both views to the Prime Minister and get her orders, because he had full confidence that I would present his views correctly before the Prime Minister on any subject. The Cabinet Secretary himself would be present along with me in very important discussions. But as one who met the Prime Minister two or three times a day, I had naturally more opportunities for discussions with her.

I had also maintained very close relations with the heads of the various Intelligence Agencies and with the Secretaries in charge of important ministries like Home, Defence and Finance. In fact, we worked as a well-knit team. There was a good deal of mutual respect and trust among us and this indeed helped a great deal in our work, particularly in those difficult days of crisis when we had to obtain quick decisions at the highest level and have them implemented, all on the strength of oral communication. Indira Gandhi had told me that I did not have to put up a note recording her decision for her formal clearance unless I myself wanted her to see such a note before the decision was conveyed to the persons concerned. However, all cases which called for detailed examination of the notes and records on the file by the Prime Minister were submitted for orders on the files.

I could see the Prime Minister any time I made a request for it, in addition to my usual morning meetings with her. She, on her own, would send for me while she would be in the midst of a discussion with a Cabinet minister or a visiting dignitary and ask me to join in the discussion, or to elucidate a particular point or carry out the follow-up action as directed by her. Similarly, I could telephone her at any time of the day or night.

Often she would send me bits of paper conveying her instructions or sometimes scribble on small note sheets suggestions for further examination. If the matter was highly sensitive or confidential, she would have such notes sealed in her presence and sent to me through her attendants. On some notes, she would scribble "Destroy after reading" and they would promptly go to the shredder behind my chair in my office. While attending meetings along with her – meetings of the cabinet, discussions with visiting delegations or just informal discussions with her cabinet colleagues – she would pass on instructions or queries on slips of paper to me and I would return them immediately with my comments or with the information she would have asked for. I myself would sometimes pass on chits to her with my comments and suggestions on the matter under discussion, if I did not want others present to know what I had to convey. In the course of meetings with foreigners or important visitors, when I was asked to be present, she would invariably invite me to express my views or give further information on any point. If I felt that she had omitted to say something important, I would pass on a chit to her inviting her attention to that point. Over a period of time, I had developed my own techniques of communication on such occasions and I could easily know whether or when she wanted me to intervene by her gestures and nods to me.

Files and notes submitted to Indira Gandhi invariably came back the next day with precise and unambiguous instructions. She used to see files, even while travelling in planes or while camping outside Delhi and therefore, her travels, which were very frequent, did not in any way affect the prompt disposal of files. Even when she was out of Delhi, I could maintain close touch with her through the hot line and never had any difficulty in obtaining her instructions on urgent matters which could not wait till her return.

"Compulsive editor"

Getting a draft statement or the draft of an important speech to be delivered by Indira Gandhi approved by her was the most difficult part of the work of the senior officers working with her, perhaps I should say the only difficult part. Sharada Prasad had to take the brunt of this trouble, as it was mainly his responsibility to get the drafts of important statements and speeches approved by her. Indira Gandhi was a great perfectionist as far as the English language was concerned and believed in the utmost economy in the use of words. Rhetorical flourishes and embellishments in the drafts were mercilessly cut out in favour of short and simple sentences. Sometimes, we felt that her editing, while improving the language, destroyed the impact, but she would insist on her own language and style to be retained. On important drafts, Sharada Prasad would consult me, and sometimes, he and I together would be called in by the Prime Minister for the exercise of revision. The revision of a draft was often a long drawn out and laborious process. I used to think that the time and attention given by Indira Gandhi to the correction of a draft were really not worth all that trouble. Sharada Prasad was a real master in drafting speeches and messages. He knew very well Indira Gandhi's style and idiom of speech and writing and his drafts always took care of her preferences and style. Still, the drafts of important documents would go through two or three revisions before they were finally approved. She would go through each sentence very carefully, examine the aptness of a phrase used, debate whether it could be substituted by a better phrase, cut out sentences which she thought were repetitive or unnecessary, add new sentences, change the order of paragraphs or of sentences within the same paragraph and finally make the text typically "Indiraise". Whatever may be the pressure of work, she always spent a lot of time on the preparation of her speeches and statements and we got the impression that in a way she enjoyed this self-inflicted rigour. She appeared to be relaxing while going through this highly time-consuming and exacting exercise. Her main difficulty was in the Hindi translation of the drafts. While she was a good platform speaker in Hindi, written Hindi was not her forte, and we could see her struggling with the pronunciation of some of the highly sanskritised phrases which the official translators would have prepared for her.

Indira Gandhi edited every draft of an important letter or message that was to be issued in her name. Sharada Prasad used to describe her as a "compulsive editor", but we all knew and Sharada always acknowledged that every draft came out better after her editing. Sometimes, she would send very important letters revised and signed by her in the final form before despatch through her Personal Assistant with a slip to me that it should be seen by me before issue. Even at that stage, she was open to suggestions for changes in the substance of the letter, if I had any suggestion to offer.

Press conferences

Indira Gandhi was invariably at her best in her press conferences. One of my important duties, particularly when I travelled with her in foreign countries, was to assist her in her press conferences. Sharada Prasad and I would go through an exercise of listing out questions which could be anticipated and discuss with her in advance the answers to such questions. I would sit next to her at all press conferences and would quietly and unostentatiously pass on factual information if she needed, on any matter that was raised. She relied on me for furnishing her with statistical and factual information on matters raised at these conferences if such information was needed by her. Over a period of time, I could correctly guess whether she wanted me to give the additional information or even to intervene with an explanation or elucidation of a point made by her. She was quite relaxed during her press conferences and always came out with apt repartees and witty comments which made these meetings very lively. She rarely lost her temper or patience even when sarcastic questions were flung at her. On the other hand, she would deal with such questions with great tact and ease and sometimes make the questioner defenceless by turning the tables on him.

Sense of humour

Indira Gandhi had a great sense of humour which was known only to those who were very close to her. She enjoyed good jokes and could narrate jokes and anecdotes with great relish. She would giggle and laugh and mimic and gesture expressively while relating her stories and it was a great pleasure watching her in a totally relaxed mood on such occasions. Sometimes, she would pass chits to me making an apt comment on something just going on before her and keep a poker face. One day, two eminent Indian scientists, whose dislike for each other was well known, were discussing with her the position India should take on the peace movements.   When she noticed that they were opposing each other rather vehemently even in her presence, she wrote on a slip of paper "these two should first learn to keep peace between them" and passed it on to me without any change of expression on her face.

At a press conference in London, within a few days of the visit of the Soviet Defence Minister, Marshal Ustinov, to India, she was asked what the tangible result of the weighty defence delegation which had visited India a few days earlier was.

She whispered to me with a solemn face "weighty indeed" alluding to the massive physical proportions of Marshal Ustinov and went on to answer that question with perfect ease. I could not help laughing at this apt comment and the television cameras caught me in this lapse fully.

Another instance of her sense of humour comes to my mind. I was travelling with her on a visit to Hyderabad and Trivandrum in July 1984. She had invited my wife also to travel in her plane. At Hyderabad, R.Venkataraman, then Defence Minister, asked me to travel in his plane to Trivandrum, which was leaving an hour earlier. I then said that my wife was resting at the Raj Bhavan and I would travel along with her later in the Prime Minister's plane. Indira Gandhi then promptly commented with mischievous laughter, "Venkataraman, don't try to persuade him. He would not like to miss his wife's company even for one hour". We all heartily joined in the laughter. Later, when we landed at Trivandrum airport and as she was leaving the reception pandal, she caught hold of my wife by both hands and told her laughing loudly: "Do you know, Alexander couldn't miss your company even for one hour?"

Indira Gandhi had a fund of anecdotes and stories and took great delight in narrating them in her intimate circle of acquaintances. While giving such anecdotes, she would often use direct tense for conversation to add flavour to the story and make them very vivid and interesting to the listeners. She once told me the story of her becoming a non-vegetarian. Her grandmother, Mrs. Motilal Nehru, wanted young Indira to grow up as a vegetarian, though the Kashmiri Pandit community generally, and all the menfolk in the Nehru family, were non-vegetarians. One evening young Indira had gone from her school to a friend's house. When she returned home, she refused to eat the dinner which the servants in Anand Bhavan had served her and insisted that she should have the same "bajji" she had eaten earlier in her friend's house. When the servants reported the situation to the senior Mrs. Nehru, she asked them to find out from the friend's house what special "bajji" had been served to the child and then make it and give it to her immediately. The grandmother soon discovered to her horror that the "bajji" that Indira ate and enjoyed thoroughly earlier was mutton cutlet. The matter was reported to Motilal Nehru, who in his wisdom advised his wife to give up trying to bring up the child as a vegetarian since she had already acquired a liking for non-vegetarian food. From then on, Indira was allowed non-vegetarian meals as in the case of the male members of the household.

Indira Gandhi as a speaker

As a speaker or debater, Indira Gandhi was at her best when she did not have to use a prepared text. Reading from a text often cramped her style of delivery, but she preferred to speak from a text on most formal occasions. While addressing political gatherings, she always spoke extempore and these speeches were some of her best. The Hindi she used on those occasions was the Hindustani of Uttar

Pradesh, with which she was quite at ease. She could easily establish a rapport with her audience and rise to great heights of eloquence in such meetings. But her delivery from a prepared text was generally flat and unimpressive except at large international gatherings where almost all speeches are read.

Indira Gandhi's television speeches were perhaps the most disappointing of her speeches. She appeared rather lifeless while reading and did not appear to be relaxed.

In the Parliament she was at her best when she was provoked by the opposition. She would then depart from the prepared text and give it hot and straight in her own forceful style.

She had the habit – very inconvenient for those responsible for drafting her speeches – of continuing to make changes in the text till the last minute. Sharada Prasad used to say that the best insurance against such changes was to get the text printed in advance. Her speech at the Conference of heads of government at Cancun, Mexico had been prepared well in advance and had undergone several revisions before we had arrived there. But after taking her seat at the conference table, she made several important changes in the text and I had the mortifying experience of watching some of the finely chiselled and polished sentences and phrases over which several hours had been spent in Delhi by some of us, being discarded at the last minute and substituted by altogether new sentences.

I would not describe Indira Gandhi as a great speaker or debater. She did not have the oratorical skills of her father who could move the audience by the style of delivery and the use of apt phrases and sentences which even now ring in the ears of the people. She was not particularly at ease in her role in Parliament. She used to prepare well for answering questions and get herself thoroughly briefed by the officers of the concerned departments at least a day before the question came up in Parliament. These briefing sessions were held in the Cabinet room adjacent to her office in Parliament House and she would go through each question and the possible supplementaries with meticulous care. She would often revise the draft answers at these meetings and ask the officers to furnish additional information for the note for pad. One of my important responsibilities as Principal Secretary was to assist the Prime Minister in preparing replies to Parliament questions and collecting information for possible supplementary questions. In spite of these thorough preparations, I always had the impression that Indira Gandhi did not feel relaxed in answering questions in Parliament.

She used to be present at Parliament during the question hour and during special discussions on confidence motions, adjournment motions, etc.; otherwise she preferred to be in her office in Parliament House most of the time. She was always present in her office in Parliament House during the entire session of Parliament and could be often seen rushing to the Lok Sabha or Rajya Sabha when her presence was suddenly required. Once when I was with her in her office she got a message that she had to be present in the House immediately. She collected her papers and made a quick dash to the Lok Sabha and I had to literally run at good speed to catch up with her. On our way back from the House to her office, I told her that she could easily beat P.T. Usha in a race. She answered with great confidence: "I can beat anyone in an over-65 veterans' race" and added with obvious relish, "men included".

Concentration of power

Indira Gandhi has often been criticised for keeping too much power in her hand and not allowing her ministers to exercise the power which normally belonged to them. From my experience of working in the Prime Minister's Office and also of my knowledge of the decision-making processes in earlier years, I should admit that far too many cases came from the ministers to the Prime Minister's Office seeking "advice", "direction", or "decision" during the 80s compared with the practice in the 60s or early 70s. One of the important reasons for this trend was the poor quality and level of competence of a few of her colleagues in the council of ministers and a few of the Chief Ministers in the States.

Indira Gandhi was very conscious of the limitations of some of her cabinet colleagues and kept a vigilant eye on their work. She used to receive reports about the inadequacies and sometimes lapses of some of these ministers; but she had a weakness for those who had loyally stood by her in times of crisis. She also had her own assessment of a person's usefulness to the party, irrespective of his efficiency as a minister. She knew the power equations within the party and who counted most and where, at the time of elections. She was also quite conscious of the intricate play of communal, caste and even sub-caste considerations at state levels and could not be easilsy persuaded to drop a minister merely on the grounds of his poor performance. One may not fully agree with her, but it was her policy to assess the usefulness of a person not mainly on the basis of his performance as a minister but also as a party man. Some inefficient ministers were extremely useful as party men and she considered it necessary to carry them in her council of ministers. Critics may say that her objectivity was clouded by party interests in the matter of choosing ministers, but she thought that some degree of inefficiency had to be tolerated for political reasons.

She was quite averse to merciless chopping off of deadwood because she did not want to humiliate any of her ministerial colleagues and thereby reduce their influence and effectiveness as party leaders. She would, in some bad cases of poor performance, shift that person to a less important charge or in some special cases push him on to a ceremonial post or sometimes a party post. She was always keen to save the face of the person concerned and would go a long way to ensure that the dropping someone from her council of ministers was not seen by the people as a personal humiliation for him.

Indira Gandhi used the meetings of the Cabinet and of the Cabinet Committees to assess the worth and capabilities of her ministerial colleagues. Sometimes, she would be visibly annoyed to see a minister coming to these meetings without thorough preparation and briefing. She did not like secretaries to government presenting their ministry's proposals at the meetings of the cabinet. In fact, she had stopped the practice of secretaries participating in the discussions at cabinet meetings. The only secretaries present at cabinet meetings were the Cabinet Secretary and the Principal Secretary to the Prime Minister. In certain meetings, the Additional Secretary to the Prime Minister would also be present. The Prime Minister allowed and even expected me to express my views freely at these meetings. However, I intervened only when I was sure that the Prime Minister wanted me to do so. Some of the ministers did not like the idea of a civil servant pointing out the deficiencies in their proposals. But what annoyed Indira Gandhi most was that some ministers came to the cabinet meetings without doing any homework, and therefore, could not properly explain their proposals before the cabinet.

Incidentally, there was an interesting background to Indira Gandhi's decision to dispense with the practice of secretaries attending the meetings of the cabinet. At one cabinet meeting, two secretaries entered into a heated argument with each other on a proposal. They talked at each other rather freely, ignoring the fact that it was a meeting of the council of ministers and not of secretaries. The secretaries are invited to be present at the meeting of the ministers only to assist their ministers or to offer clarifications and explanations when called upon to do so. They cannot appropriate for themselves the role of participants. Even if they participate in a discussion, they have always to remember that it is a meeting of the ministers and to maintain the circumspection expected of a civil servant on such occasions. Indira Gandhi was not pleased with the conduct of the two secretaries and stopped the practice of secretaries attending cabinet meetings. Secretaries were, however, asked to be present in the room near the cabinet room to be called in if their presence was found necessary. On a few occasions some of them were invited to answer some queries or clarify some points.

Some ministers used to send files to the Prime Minster's Office with a note saying, "PM may also kindly see before orders are issued". Some others would refer all cases of nominations to Committees and Boards and ask for the Prime Minister's "guidance". Some ministers would send the drafts of the statements they were to make in Parliament to be cleared in advance by her. A few who did not have confidence in their own judgement, thought it advisable to obtain the Prime Minister's orders even on matters where such orders were not necessary, thereby adding to the workload of the Prime Minister. Since the Prime Minister herself had reservations on the abilities of some of her colleagues, she did not discourage this practice and thought that this was one way of keeping control on their functioning. But this became a regular practice with some ministers and this brought into the functioning of the Central Government a new practice of ministers voluntarily subjecting their decision-making powers to the authority of the Prime Minister even in cases when it was quite unnecessary.

The Cabinet Committee on Political Affairs is the most important body which the Prime Minister consults on all major policy matters. During the Punjab agitation, this Committee used to meet very frequently and sometimes even twice a day. All major matters relating to defence, including major defence purchases were placed before this Committee. The membership of this Committee was limited to four or five senior cabinet colleagues and discussions were very frank and informal. The Cabinet Secretary and I attended all its meetings and were encouraged to express our views freely on all matters which came up for consideration. Sometimes, the Committee met without a formal agenda or background notes. The Prime Minister would bring up specific subjects for discussion and invite the views of the members.

While Indira Gandhi encouraged her cabinet colleagues to express their views freely and frankly at the meetings of the cabinet and its committees, some ministers preferred not to risk the chance of a difference of opinion on any issue with her. Perhaps these ministers thought that what the Prime Minister expected from them was full compliance with her views and not frank expression of their own views. She had often expressed deep disappointment at the absence of constructive criticism and suggestions from some of her cabinet colleagues. Some were willing to leave all important decisions to Indira Gandhi. Most of them treated her not as a colleague or first among equals, but as someone whose decisions they should accept unquestioningly, whatever might be their own views on the issues involved.

Indira Gandhi often consulted some of her senior cabinet colleagues, particularly R. Venkataraman and P.V. Narasimha Rao, individually on sensitive and important issues even before they were formally brought up for consideration before the cabinet. She would also sound a few trusted advisers informally before taking a definite position on some issues. The choice of the advisers would depend on the subject. This circle of advisers included G. Parthasarathy, L.K. Jha and Pupul Jayakar. On important political issues she would consult leaders like Kamalapathi Tripathi and Uma Shankar Dikshit. She knew the strong points of her advisers and sought their views on matters where she believed their advice would be helpful in making up her mind. Sometimes, there would be informal meetings at her residence attended by two or three of her cabinet colleagues and some of her advisers.

These elaborate consultations with a large number of persons enabled her to know all sides of a problem. But the ultimate decision was her own and she took full responsibility for these decisions, whether they were made in consultation with a large number of colleagues or by the Cabinet Committee on Political Affairs. In spite of the fact that Indira Gandhi was held in great respect, if not awe, by most of her cabinet colleagues, these individual consultations encouraged some of them to speak out their minds more boldly than would be the case in the forum of the cabinet or a cabinet committee.

Indira Gandhi had her own techniques and style for these consultations. She would not inform any person about the views expressed by others. Sometimes, she would casually mention a subject to a colleague or a trusted adviser and see how he reacted off hand. Sometimes, she would mention to me the views expressed by one of her ministers or advisers on a particular subject and if I expressed a different view or brought in a new point, she would ask me to discuss it with that person again and report to her.

A common criticism about Indira Gandhi's style of working was that she did not give much importance to the views expressed by her colleagues either in the Party or in the government. This is an undeserved criticism. The trouble on the other hand was that some of her colleagues in the government or the Party did not express their views frankly and strongly and were instead willing and ready to be "guided" or "advised" by her. Of course, Indira Gandhi did not hesitate to overrule her ministers when she found that they had taken wrong or indefensible decisions.

On important matters relating to the Party in the States, Indira Gandhi often accommodated the views of some of her senior colleagues in the cabinet. In matters like selection of Pradesh Congress Chiefs or leaders of Congress Legislature Parties, she would give weight to the views of the senior ministers, though she had always to take the blame herself, if the selection turned out to be unpopular. The senior ministers, some of whom had also senior positions in the Party, were invariably consulted by her on all issues which were likely to affect the interests of the Party. I could see that she attached a good deal of importance to their advice on what she considered as Party issues.

Cabinet reshuffles

While discussing Indira Gandhi's style of functioning, some observations about her style of reshuffling her cabinets will be in order. Indira Gandhi never followed the technique of a clean sweep or even a major shake-up and, therefore, her exercise in cabinet changes generally became non-events. She believed in marginal changes and shifts and could not therefore, create any deep impact on the psychology or mood of the people through these changes.

The first major change in the cabinet after I joined her office was in January 1982. Whenever she thought of making changes in the cabinet, I was one of the first who would be taken into confidence. She would ask me first to do an exercise on the reorganisation of the departments and ministries, taking into account the experience of the working of different ministries, and particularly the load of work with the ministers. She would give some indications if she herself felt that a particular ministry had become too unwieldy or a particular subject required better attention at political levels. I used to conduct this exercise secretly without giving any hint to any one that a reorganisation of work among the ministers was in the offing. I would prepare charts indicating suggestions as to which subjects should appropriately be grouped under which ministry, which ministry should appropriately have cabinet level ministers and how many ministers of State or deputy ministers would be required for different ministries. She would discuss these charts with me in great detail and finally take her decision on the reorganised set up along with the decision as to who should be in charge of which ministry. Sometimes, the principles followed in reorganisation would get compromised to accommodate the background of the minister eventually chosen for a particular position.

Indira Gandhi rarely consulted any of her senior cabinet colleagues about the changes she proposed to make in the cabinet or even about the deputy ministers or ministers of State who were to work with them. In fact, often the ministers, including her seniormost colleagues came to know about the changes in their portfolios or induction of new faces only a little before the time fixed for swearing in.

In spite of her reputation for ruthlessness in dealing with her colleagues, she was never really ruthless in the manner of dropping or shifting her colleagues. Bhishma Narayan Singh and A.P.

Sharma were offered governorships when she decided to drop them from the cabinet. Kedar Nath Pandey was shifted to Irrigation from an important portfolio like Railways when she decided to revamp the Railway administration. P.C. Sethi was given the charge of Planning Commission and later given additional charge of Irrigation when he was shifted from Home. C.M. Stephen was given an important party post when he resigned from the cabinet. She did not have the heart to make any of her senior colleagues feel humiliated.

I remember the mental torture Indira Gandhi had in informing R. Venkataraman that she would like to shift him from Finance to Defence. Indira Gandhi had made up her mind to appoint Pranab Mukherjee as Finance minister but felt very reluctant about breaking the news to R. Venkataraman, thinking that he might feel that he was being demoted. She asked me on a few occasions whether Venkataraman would feel hurt if he were shifted to Defence. The Prime Minister had been holding additional charge of Defence for a year and badly wanted to be relieved of this extra burden. She thought Venkataraman most suitable to take on this sensitive assignment, particularly as she had confidence in his ability to maintain good relations with the Chiefs of Staff and to curb the trend of making excessive demands on the budget. I would not say that she had equally high concern about the feelings of all other colleagues, but she had always held R. Venkataraman in high esteem and was anxious that he should not have any bad feelings about this change. Finally, Venkataraman was told about the proposed change a day before the swearing in and he expressed his readiness to take on Defence with great enthusiasm. The Prime Minister was quite relieved at this development.

R. Venkataraman took to his work in the Defence ministry with such interest and involvement that he was in fact not quite enthusiastic when two years later the Prime Minister informed him of her wish to field him as candidate for the post of Vice-President. The Prime Minister talked to him about this at the Defence Research Laboratory, Hyderabad, on 19 July 1984 where she had gone for a Defence ministry function. I accompanied her on this visit. I was aware that she had made up her mind to offer the Vice-Presidentship to Venkataraman, but had not found a suitable opportunity for mentioning it to him till then. We were having tea at the *shamiana* and I reminded her that there were only a few days left for filing the nomination for the Vice-President's post. She then moved on to where Venkataraman was standing with some officers and took him aside and informed him of her proposal. She came back in a few minutes to where I was standing and told me that Venkataraman was so happy with his work in the Defence ministry that he was not very excited at the prospect of becoming Vice-President. He, however, told her that if it was her wish that he should be proposed as the candidate for Vice-President, he would of course accept it. I mention these episodes to show how solicitous she was about the feelings of some of her cabinet colleagues and how reluctant she was to force her decisions on them.

In the January 1982 cabinet changes, the Prime Minister had thought of appointing G. Parthasarathi as the minister for Commerce in place of Pranab Mukherjee, but only with a minister of State rank. The cabinet list which included several changes had been prepared on that basis. G. Parthasarathi was called in to her office in the South Block on the morning of the date of the swearing in ceremony and told about her decision. I was waiting in the Special Assistant's room next to the Prime Minister's office and I saw Parthasarathi coming out of her office within a couple of minutes of entering it. He had straightaway declined the offer and there was no attempt on Indira Gandhi's part to persuade him either. She called me in and said that GP was not interested in becoming a minister and added that probably GP was not satisfied with the rank of minister of State that had been offered to him, though it was to be an independent charge. I do not know whether GP would have been happy even with a cabinet rank. He is one of the very few I have known with a definite dislike for any ministerial post. He always preferred to work from behind the scenes rather than from the centre-stage. The decision to shift Shivraj Patil, Minister of State for Defence, to Commerce, was taken within a minute of knowing GP's reaction and appropriate changes were made in the letter to the President at the proverbial eleventh hour before the swearing in ceremony.

Indira Gandhi heartily disliked lobbying by any aspirant or any pressure group for ministerial positions and that was the main reason for her dealing with cabinet changes with the utmost secrecy. I was the only person, besides one or two within her personal office, involved in preparing the papers, who would be taken into confidence about cabinet changes. She allowed me full ɔ express my views on the candidates proposed for inclusion in the cabinet. Indira Gandhi knew that I would never canvass support for any friend or clique and that whatever observations I made were always on the strict criterion of what I considered to be merits. She also knew that I would never divulge the information to anyone. In order to avoid the possibility of leakage of news, the letter to the President was typed and despatched only an hour or two before the swearing in. President Sanjiva Reddy was particular that he should be informed about any cabinet changes well in advance. Indira Gandhi would sometimes call on the President and mention to him the important changes she proposed to make and send the final letter to him only few hours before the swearing in ceremony. In almost all cases, the press and sometimes the ministers themselves came to know of the changes only at the swearing in ceremony at Rashtrapati Bhavan. R.K. Dhawan had the main responsibility for arranging the typing and despatch of the letters to the President. Indira Gandhi used to ask him or Fotedar to inform the persons to be newly sworn in as ministers to be present at Rashtrapati Bhavan just an hour or so before the swearing in. In some cases, she herself would talk to the person concerned. Even the Cabinet Secretary, who was responsible for making arrangements for the swearing in function, would know about the changes only an hour or two before the ceremony.

Budget exercise

In the formulation of the annual budget, both the Railway and the general budget, the minister concerned would have a few rounds of discussions with the Prime Minister to obtain her guidance and instructions. She viewed the budget not merely as an accounting or financial exercise, but as an instrument for implementing her policies and would judge every proposal on the criterion whether it fulfilled the broad policy objectives of the Party. She had asked me to attend the important discussions on the budget proposals which the Finance Minister used to have with his officers and I would keep her fully informed of the trend of these discussions. Indira Gandhi had an uncanny feel for what affected the common people and would not easily allow proposals which she felt would harm their interests. Economics was not Mrs Gandhi's strong point, but her political antenna was so sensitive that she would instinctively know which economic proposal was likely to harm the interests of the common people and would take a bold and uncompromising stand on such proposals, whatever might be the collective wisdom of economic pundits and bureaucrats or the insistence of the minister concerned.

Mastery over foreign policy issues

If I am asked to identify two strong points and two major handicaps in Indira Gandhi's working, I shall list her mastery of India's foreign policy and her sound and mature political judgement as her strong points, and her basic distrust of colleagues and her sense of loneliness as her handicaps.

As one who had several occasions to watch her talking to world leaders and taking decisions on important foreign policy issues, I would say without hesitation that she was a greater expert on these issues than any minister or civil servant in the Government of India in the 80s. Of course, she had the rare advantage of having been trained by her father, the original author and authentic interpreter of India's foreign policy, and of observing him dealing with foreign dignitaries and foreign policy issues. But she had brought into this rich experience and background a distinctive personal style of grace of her own which earned for her a well-deserved reputation as the most effective exponent of India's foreign policy. She knew what to say and what not to say and how to say and how much to say to friends and foes alike during her meetings with high level foreign dignitaries. Every sentence was carefully articulated and every phrase was aptly selected. There would be very little emotion, rancour or bitterness even when discussing extremely unpleasant subjects with heads of government with whom India's relations were not cordial. Her pauses and silences, deliberate under-statements, non-committal responses and counter-questions on certain occasions showed what a skilful diplomat she was. She kept herself within the broad parameters of foreign policy laid down by her father and used her friendship with world leaders to explain India's stand on various issues and to carve out for India a position of respect and importance.

If one recalls the position of India at the time of her return to power in early 1980 and that at the close of 1984, one will be able to make a correct appraisal of her contribution in once again making India one of the most respected countries of the world. During the three years of the Janata government, their advocacy and practice of foreign policy based on the ill-defined doctrine of "genuine non-alignment" had practically reduced India to being ignored by friends and foes alike. The persistent anti-Indira propaganda which the Janata government had carried on in foreign countries had given India the distorted image of a Soviet client. Some important western politicians who had glibly swallowed this line of propaganda had almost written off Indira Gandhi as a Soviet fellow-traveller by the time she was returned to power in 1980 and her declarations on India's adherence to non-alignment were treated with cynical disbelief. But by skilful diplomatic moves and deft handling of delicate foreign policy issues, she earned the respect and confidence of the western world's top leaders. Her visits to the U.K., U.S.A., France and the Scandinavian countries and meetings with a large number of eminent intellectuals and political leaders helped project the correct image of India and even Reagan's U.S.A. was willing to acknowledge Indira Gandhi and India as the authentic champion of the non-aligned and developing world. Simultaneously, she kept Indo-Soviet relations at a level of mutual respect and understanding and the Soviet leaders came to accept non-aligned India as a source of strength and stability in a divided world.

The acme of her success in the field of India's international relations came when Indira Gandhi was elected chairperson of the Non-Aligned Movement in 1983. It was Iraq's turn to host this meeting, but because of the continuing Iran-Iraq war, a new venue and chairman had to be found. Indira Gandhi's prestige was so great in the non-aligned world that she became the unanimous choice for chairmanship and Delhi earned the privilege of being the venue of the Conference. The personal charm and diplomatic skills Indira Gandhi showed while chairing the long sessions of the NAM in New Delhi elicited for her and India unstinted praise and respect and India once again emerged as the unquestioned voice of the Third World.

Loneliness and tendency to mistrust others

Indira Gandhi was one of the loneliest leaders in contemporary history. In spite of the adulation of millions of her countrymen which was generously showered on her and the unquestioned trust and loyalty extended to her by her colleagues in the Party and the Government, she remained lonely and always conscious of her loneliness. I always had the feeling that she never trusted any person completely or unreservedly. Perhaps, some of the explanations for this trait in her personality should be sought in her childhood and family background. Part of this trait can be attributed to the very bitter experiences she had to go through during the 1977-79 period. Some people who had known her very closely for long years have told that her mistrust of others became pronounced only after 1977.

Indira Gandhi's childhood was an unusually lonely one. In spite of the affection and doting care she enjoyed in generous measure from her grandparents and parents, as a child, she lived a lonely life in that large family. With a father in and out of the jail, a mother always in poor health and without the close companionship of children of her age, Indira spent her early years almost all by herself. She considered her father's sisters too dominating and, therefore, she was not particularly fond of their company. Vijayalakshmi Pandit's cold and condescending attitude to Kamala Nehru had created in young Indira's mind deep disappointment, if not resentment, regarding the elder female members of the family and made her life even more lonely.

As the chief hostess in Jawaharlal Nehru's household, Indira had met and entertained a large number of eminent Indians and world leaders, but she always remained alone and somewhat aloof. The premature death of her husband, Feroze Gandhi, and the sudden death of her father who was her friend, philosopher and guide and father and mother rolled into one had aggravated her loneliness in her middle life. The cruellest blow was yet to come, and that was the untimely death of Sanjay Gandhi in very tragic circumstances. With Sanjay's death she lost a strong pillar of understanding and support in her public life and she withdrew herself deeper into a shell. Then came an equally bitter blow and that was the decision of Maneka to leave the house and also take away Varun, the infant grandson, from her house and worse still, not to send the child to see her even for one day in a month. It was mortifying for the grandmother who doted on this child to be denied the pleasure of meeting him, but she accepted this as another of the great personal tragedies which she had to live with and this added to the poignancy of her loneliness. Sonia Gandhi, whom I would name as the one person for whom Indira Gandhi had unreserved trust and respect, had been making sincere efforts to lighten the bitterness of the personal tragedies in her life and had succeeded to a large extent. This young woman of Italian birth and upbringing was more than what any affectionate typical Indian daughter would have been to a mother and proved to be a source of great comfort and support to Indira in her family life, particularly in the last few years of serious tensions and crisis.

The bitter experience of 1977, 1978 and 1979 which Indira Gandhi had to go through were something which very few people of her background and position had ever to face in life. It was not so much the persecution by her opponents through inquiry commissions, arrests, expulsion from Parliament, etc., that tormented this sensitive woman, as the attitude of some of her erstwhile friends and followers towards her after her fall from power. Suddenly, these people stopped visiting her or talking to her. Some of them who used to be regular visitors to 1 Safdarjung Road – though they could not often meet Mrs Gandhi, they were quite happy in marking attendance in Dhawan's room or standing at a convenient place to catch her eye as she walked to her office – suddenly stopped their visits after she lost power and moved to her new residence at Willingdon Crescent. They were scared that they would be noticed by the intelligence men and their visits reported to the new bosses in the government who were keeping a vigilant watch on her. Some of them pretended that they had never known her while some others joined the campaign of personal vilification against her with the zeal of new converts. What was significant was that some of the political leaders who deserted her and became her bitter critics were persons who never would have had any place in Indian politics but for her patronage and support. Persons whom she had trusted and helped and who came up in life climbing the political ladder she extended to them were now vying with each other to proclaim what a fiend they had been serving and became more severe critics of her than her life-long political adversaries. The crass ingratitude on the part of those who had earlier benefited from her and the indifference and coldness of those who till her fall were proud to be known as followers, deeply shook her faith in values like friendship and loyalty and made her lonelier than before.

After Indira Gandhi's return to power in 1980, she took back most of those who had deserted her in the hour of crisis, including some who had gone out of their way to malign her. But I do not think she easily forgot these experiences because she would on certain occasions recall with great bitterness what some of them who were now working closely with her or in high positions in her government and the Party had said or done during those difficult years. She had forgiven generously, but could not so easily forget.

During the early months of my service with Indira Gandhi, I was somewhat formal in my relations with her, venturing to give my views and suggestions strictly on official matters. But very soon, she made it clear to me that she expected me to give my views and suggestions on everything with which she was concerned. She would freely talk to me about her Party affairs, the strong and weak points of her cabinet and Party colleagues, who let her down and how at a crucial stage or crisis, the reports she had received about corrupt practices of some of her trusted colleagues, the information she had come across on the personal lives of some prominent persons in public life, the influences exerted by certain businessmen on some political leaders and also about donations received by some leaders in the name of Party but which had not reached the Party in full. She encouraged me to express my views on all major appointments to civil, military and political posts with the full confidence that I would not project my personal likes and dislikes in such matters and that my suggestions would be in what I considered the best interests of the Prime Minister and the country. She often used me as a testing ground on what the average Indian would think of any proposal objectively and encouraged me to express my views freely even when I knew that she held totally different views on the subject. On some occasions, she would freely express her fears and anxieties about a particular situation or individual and I could see that sometimes in the loneliness of her great position she was speaking out in an exercise to find relief for her tensions.

I vividly recall her sense of deep displeasure and frustration after the results of the Assembly elections in Haryana, Himachal

Pradesh, Kerala and West Bengal and of seven crucial by-elections to the Parliament in May 1982. She had done vigorous campaigning for the Assembly elections and had thrown her full weight and prestige in canvassing support for the Congress candidates. But the reverses suffered by the Congress in these elections and the loss of some prestigious parliamentary seats came as a rude shock to her. Everywhere, she found the party ridden by factions and in-fighting and she was upset by the reports about some Congressmen working against Congress candidates. Some Congressmen seemed to believe that winning elections for them was the sole responsibility of Indira Gandhi and if the Party fared badly it was a matter for her to worry about.

In this mood of deep personal disappointment, she seriously considered giving up her responsibilities as Party President and Prime Minister and offering herself as a candidate for the post of President for which elections were to be held in two months. On several occasions in May 1982, she seriously discussed this proposal with me. "Haven't I done enough for the Party and shouldn't I now hand over the burden to others?" She asked me once in great mental agony. She believed that the Party had got into a mood of complacency and lethargy and needed a shock treatment which could be administered by her quitting as Party President and Prime Minister. She said that she wanted some time for rest and writing, which the Rashtrapati Bhavan could provide, and her advice to a new government would still be available in her capacity as President. I knew she was talking seriously and not merely testing my reaction to a hypothetical proposition, as she used to do on other issues and that she had been so deeply disturbed at the state of affairs in the Party that she would really go in for a shock treatment of this type. I argued with her that the country needed her leadership for at least another term as Prime Minister and that if she left the post of Prime Minister at that stage, the country would be thrown back to chaos and confusion and the chances of a recovery might irretrievably be lost. I also said that destiny had assigned to her this role at a very crucial period in the country's history and that the shock treatment of the type she had in view might result in the collapse of the Party and the government. I knew she was disgusted with the pettiness, corruption and in-fighting she saw among some of her party men, but she also knew that she could not easily shed the tremendous responsibility which fate had placed upon her. I fully sympathised with her plight, more so, because I knew she could not even seriously discuss these thoughts with her party men or cabinet colleagues and had to resolve her inner conflicts and doubts all by herself. Indira Gandhi had tremendous reserves of mental strength and will power to draw upon in a crisis. This is what she did, and I found that she had bounced back to optimism and enthusiasm in a matter of days.

Handling crisis situations

Very soon Mrs Gandhi had to go through much greater mental anguish. The senseless killings of innocent persons by Sikh extremists in Punjab and the mass murders in Assam had deeply disturbed her and caused her tremendous mental distress, but I found that far from getting frustrated, she became all the more convinced that she had to carry on with greater vigour the fight for the country's integrity and unity. On all such occasions, she remained firm in her conviction that she had to lead the fight.

Indira Gandhi had the unusual gift of dealing with crisis and calamity with all the seriousness they deserved and quickly switching her mind on to something totally different and feeling relaxed the next minute. While some of us working closely with her carried the tensions of a crisis round the clock into whatever else we handled, she could move from a serious crisis meeting of Punjab or Assam to a meeting on wildlife or leprosy eradication for example, with perfect ease, totally banishing the subject of the crisis from her mind.

Maximum use of time

Those who have watched Indira Gandhi at work closely would have noticed her skill and capacity to be alert and active while handling two or three tasks simultaneously. While presiding over a meeting of the Cabinet Committee on Political Affairs or having discussions with her cabinet colleagues on a serious subject, she could simultaneously be revising the draft of a speech or going through the mail in the folders in front of her. A telephone call to someone on a totally different subject could also fit into this schedule. She had mastered this technique of attending to two or three things simultaneously so well that she could make the maximum use of her time at her disposal. Even while covering the short distance from her house to the office, she would use the time in the car to read a letter or a few pages of a book.

It was indeed remarkable that a person so busy as Indira Gandhi could find any time for reading. Occasionally, she would mention to me something interesting she had read in a book the previous night and when I once asked her how she found the time for reading, her reply was: "If you really want to do a thing, you will always find the time for it". She read more books than most of us who worked with her, though she spent more time working than many of us. She often told me that four hours sleep was more than adequate for a healthy person of her age and five hours would be a luxury. But unlike many others of her age, she did not have to spend any time trying to go to sleep. She could fall asleep whenever she wanted to.

Her eating habits and ability to relax in times of stress and crisis contributed to a great extent to her remarkably good health. In spite of a rigorous and gruelling schedule of seventeen to eighteen hours a day, she was never tired even at the age of 67. She never overate and was always conscious of any extra intake of calories which might add to her weight. She used to skip her meals on Mondays, not for any religious reason, but, as she said, for giving a rest to her system. If she had to attend a banquet or host one on a Monday, she would fast on some other day.

Her dress was always simple and neat. She wore no gold ornaments or rings and always appeared elegant and graceful whether in a white khadi saree or in rich Kancheepuram silk. Elegance and tidiness, simplicity and charm were indeed the most outstanding features of her personality.

3

TRAVELS ABROAD WITH INDIRA GANDHI

1981

Switzerland, Kuwait and U.A.E.: 5-13 May 1981

Indira Gandhi had been out of power for three years and during this period her political adversaries had been carrying on a vilification campaign against her in foreign countries, making her out to be a cruel dictator and the destroyer of India's infant democracy. Her views or statements received very little notice in foreign media during this period and a highly distorted image of her, therefore, had been built up in the west. Further, there had been several changes in heads of government and she had no opportunity of meeting some of the new leaders. She felt the need for establishing personal contact at heads of government level and also explaining to the western media personally what actually had happened in India in the years immediately preceding the Emergency and later in the Janata period. She had received a large number of invitations for visits from various heads of government and international organisations and she decided to undertake a few foreign visits from May 1981, i.e. nearly a year and a half after her return to power.

Her first visits to Switzerland, Kuwait and the United Arab Emirates (U.A.E.), were to start within three days of my taking over as Principal Secretary.

During the period of my service with Indira Gandhi, she had undertaken State visits on over a dozen occasions, some visits covering three or four countries. I was a member of her team on all these visits except on one or two when I had to stay back for other urgent government business. On most of these visits she did not include Foreign Minister, P.V. Narasimha Rao in her delegations.

She had great regard and respect for Narasimha Rao's knowledge of foreign policy issues and his capacity to be able to explain India's stand to outsiders. However, she herself was an expert on foreign policy matters and did not really need the assistance or advice from either the Foreign Minister or other experts in the ministry of External Affairs. She would hold briefings a day or two before the visit of an important foreign dignitary or delegation or before her own visit to a foreign country. But in most of these she would explain the nuances of our foreign policy to the experts in the Ministry of External Affairs or in her own office rather than be briefed by them.

During discussions with heads of foreign governments, she needed very little assistance on political issues from anyone accompanying her. On bilateral economic relations or on international economic issues, she generally asked me to do the talking, intervening occasionally to emphasise or annotate some point. As a result of my experience of participating in such discussions, I knew when to pick up the thread and intervene with my comments and there was excellent understanding between us on this matter. Sometimes, some officers in her team committed the indiscretion of making comments out of turn or giving long-winded explanations and she knew how to cut short such interventions without appearing to be snubbing anyone.

My first visit abroad accompanying the Prime Minister was to Geneva, a city I had left only five days earlier. At Geneva, her main engagement was addressing the World Health Assembly on the 6th of May. It is customary for the World Health Organisation (WHO) to invite important heads of government to address its Assembly and Indira Gandhi had accepted the invitation of Dr. Mahler, the Director-General, who was personally known to her. The WHO's large assembly hall was packed to capacity long before Mrs. Gandhi arrived and several delegates and invitees could only get standing space. This was Indira Gandhi's first public exposure to a world audience since her return to power in 1980 and we could notice the tremendous interest by the media in her visit. As one who had lived in Geneva for three years, I had watched the visits of several heads of governments to the various international organisations located in that town. Many of these visits would not even get a scanty mention in the local press. In sharp contrast, Mrs. Gandhi's visit became a great media event in Geneva.

One of the highlights of Indira Gandhi's visit to Switzerland was a brief visit to her old school at Bex where she had been a boarder. For the school children and the Catholic nuns in charge of this institution, it was a big day. They assembled in the front courtyard and sang the school song with great gusto. Indira Gandhi planted a tree in the school premises to mark her visit.

Our next halt was Kuwait, which had a large number of Indians workers. We reached Kuwait from Geneva and received a spectacular welcome from the government and the people. A large crowd of Indians had come to the airport waving the Indian flag. To the ruler and his cabinet colleagues, receiving a woman head of government was an unusual experience, but with her informal manner, Mrs. Gandhi soon made them feel quite at ease. At the lunch hosted by the Emir on 10 May only half-a-dozen of the senior cabinet colleagues were present, and I was quite impressed by the warmth and respect shown to the Prime Minister by these Sheikhs dressed in their immaculate white flowing robes. I was amused to see the hosts at the lunch one by one moving towards her to be photographed with her.

The visit to Abu Dhabi, Dubai and Sharjah was like a visit by Indira Gandhi to any Indian town. The entire population of these places, Arab and Indian, appeared to turn up wherever she went taking positions on either side of the road and cheered her with great excitement waving the Indian flag and her photograph.

In the discussions Indira Gandhi had with her hosts in these countries she explained in great detail her efforts to establish friendly relations with Pakistan and how important it was for India to have a peaceful and prosperous Pakistan as her neighbour. Instability and weakness in Pakistan, she pointed out, were not in India's interest. She explained how she had unilaterally announced cease-fire after the surrender of the Pakistan army in Dacca in 1971. She took this decision because India had no territorial ambitions in Pakistan or in any of her neighbours. She believed that this gesture had been appreciated by the common people of Pakistan. Indira Gandhi's talks helped a great deal in countering the mischievous propaganda which had been launched in these countries by Pakistan against Indians in general and Mrs. Gandhi's in particular and led to the building of new bridges of understanding and co-operation among India and these countries.

The ruler of Sharjah presented her with a big sword as a token of respect to a friendly visitor. A foreign correspondent mentioned to me that it was somewhat incongruous that a sword should be gifted this frail lady but I explained to him that a sword was intended to be a tribute to her courage and the fact that she was a woman did not make any difference to the appropriateness of the gift.

The image which the Sheikhs in these countries earlier had of Indira Gandhi was that of an imperious woman, reserved and overbearing, but when they met her they found her to be a totally different person. They were greatly impressed by her informal and pleasant manners and her extremely courteous demeanour.

Kenya : 9-14 August, 1981

I next travelled abroad as a member of the Prime Minister's delegation to Kenya from 9-14 August 1981. Indira Gandhi had a longstanding invitation from President Moi to visit Kenya. The UN authorities had also invited her to address the UN conference on new and renewable sources of energy, a subject on which India had done a good deal of pioneering work. A few other heads of government had also been invited to address this conference, which was to be held at Nairobi. The Prime Minister's party included her daughter-in-law Maneka Gandhi and her grandchildren, Rahul and Priyanka. This was the first occasion I had of watching the behaviour and attitude of Maneka as a member of Indira Gandhi's family at close quarters.

The Prime Minister had a wide range of discussions on bilateral matters with President Moi and his cabinet colleagues. Other visitors to Nairobi who met her included Kurt Waldheim, Secretary-General of the United Nations, Prime Minister Trudeau of Canada and Mr and Mrs Marcos of Philippines. Mrs Marcos, who came to see her, extended a warm invitation to the Prime Minister on behalf of the President to visit Philippines, which she accepted.

The arrangements for the Prime Minister's visit in Kenya made by the Indian High Commission, showed lack of imagination to say the least. Rahul and Priyanka were supposed to be looked after by Maneka when Indira Gandhi was busy with her official engagements, but I found Maneka often in a sulking mood. She behaved as if she herself needed looking after by others. The High

Commission had badly messed up the programmes of visit for the children and was negligent in attending to even their elementary comforts in the guest house in which they were staying. Indira Gandhi had to personally attend to these small matters and give instructions directly to the Kenyan officials in charge of the visit on how the children's programmes should be arranged, what food should be served, etc. I found her in a very angry mood on the morning after our arrival when she had to spell out to the High Commissioner what things should have been taken care of in advance for the visit of a large delegation. I felt that the High Commission should have shown greater imagination and care in preparing for the visit of a Prime Minister.

I could see a lot of Mrs Gandhi as a caring and affectionate grandmother during this visit. She would personally attend to the smallest detail concerning the children, including their dress, food, sight-seeing, etc., and did her best to make them enjoy their visit. At the game park for wild animals which we visited, the grandmother in her took great delight in telling the children about the different animals and their habits and proved to be more knowledgeable on these subjects than the professional guides who were escorting us. Mrs Gandhi was extremely fond and proud of her grand-children. On various occasions she had told me with great happiness about Varun's interest in mechanical gadgets or Priyanka's expertise in making cakes. In the midst of all her official preoccupations she always remained a typical grandmother to her grand-children.

We returned to Delhi on 14 August. There was the usual scene at the airport – a large number of central ministers, Party men and Chief Ministers and ministers from neighbouring states with garlands and bouquets, vying with each other to demonstrate their respect for her. If you want to see the unabashed sycophancy of Indian politicians, the best place to watch it is the airport when the Prime Minister leaves on a foreign tour or returns from one. Indira Gandhi herself had given repeated instructions against the waste of time by so many VIPs on the ritual of seeing her off or welcoming her, but this did not deter them from thronging to the airport on all such occasions.

Jakarta, Fiji, Tonga, Australia, Philippines
23 September – 9 October 1981

Within six weeks of her return from Kenya, Indira Gandhi was again on a foreign tour, this time covering five countries in sixteen days. This visit was the longest which she had undertaken during the period of my service with her. It was during this visit that I noticed how well organised a person Indira Gandhi was in her daily routine. In each of these places, her days were packed with engagements, one following the other with hardly a few minutes in between for rest or change of dress. But on every occasion, she would be punctual to the second, looking fresh and relaxed though some members of her entourage found it a problem to keep up with her schedule. She had told me that she always personally attended to the packing of her suitcases and she did it well ahead of the date of departure. She would even decide in advance what saree she should wear on what occasion and place them in the suitcase in the strict order of her different engagements so that all that she had to do was to pick up the top saree from the suitcase every time without having to completely unpack the suitcase. She personally decided what gifts she should give to each person and took great care about the special tastes and interests of the people concerned while choosing the gifts.

Our first halt in this long tour was Jakarta. There was a glittering banquet on the day we arrived hosted by President Suharto and a *Ramayana* ballet was staged for our entertainment at the end of the banquet. The Indonesian Hanuman did a lot of modern-style jumping around and clowning and we were more amused than impressed.

Sonia Gandhi accompanied the Prime Minister on this visit and her self-effacing manner and low profile style were noted appreciatively by the members of the delegation and the hosts alike. She always avoided the cameras and disliked over zealous officials fussing around her or showing her any special deference or consideration as the Prime Minister's daughter-in-law. Her modesty was part of her personality and so, came quite naturally to her.

There were no ministers in our delegation and as the seniormost official accompanying the Prime Minister, I had the responsibility of leading the bilateral talks with the ministers and senior officials of the countries we visited. While I conducted the official level talks with the Indonesians, the Prime Minister and President Suharto had a long meeting in another room without any aides. Very often Indira Gandhi preferred meeting other heads of government at least for an hour, without aides. She found these meetings very useful and necessary in establishing a personal rapport with her counterparts. India and Indonesia had been very close to each other in the balmy days of Nehru-Sukarno friendship but the relationship had cooled considerably in subsequent years Sukarno was a fallen god by the time we visited Jakarta, but the new government which was firmly in the saddle appeared to be very sincere in its desire to strengthen Indo-Indonesian friendship and co-operation. Indira Gandhi's visit helped a great deal in re-establishing close ties of friendship and co-operation between the two countries.

Fiji

Mrs Gandhi's two-day visit to Fiji was a memorable one in many respects. The magnificent reception she received wherever she travelled in that country made us feel that we were accompanying her on a visit to an Indian state − the same rapturous crowds lining the streets, enthusiastic people running along either side of the Prime Minister's car, wild cheering, bouquets and flowers thrown at her and mothers thrusting their children for her to fondle. For the Fijians of Indian origin this was the fulfilment of a long-cherished dream. They had heard and read a great deal about Indira Gandhi but for most of them this was their first opportunity of seeing her. Indira Gandhi herself was deeply touched by the warmth and spontaneity of the welcome by Fiji's Indian community.

Suva, the capital, impressed me as a remarkably clean city, unlike any that one sees outside Europe and North America. In fact, the city looked typically European in architecture, and lay-out of the roads. But for the black and brown faces of the people one had the feeling of being in a small European town.

Mrs Gandhi stayed in the Governor-General's house while other members of her delegation stayed in a city hotel. When I visited the Governor-General's house, I was immediately struck by the 'Britishness' of the whole atmosphere. On the mantlepiece of the main sitting room, there were framed photographs of Queen

Elizabeth, Prince Philip and Prince Charles. From a wall, a large portrait of King George V stared at me, transporting me back to the pre-war years of imperial rule. The Fijians appeared to be genuinely proud of their British connection, particularly in claiming Elizabeth II as their own Queen, which according to their Constitution she was. What struck me most was that there were no portraits or photographs of any Fijian leader in that room. Perhaps Fiji is one of the few countries in the world with no national heroes. There has been no freedom fighter in its history because it did not have to fight for its independence; it was given to it by the British. In fact, the Fijians had earlier invited the British to take over the country and rule over them and have been quite happy and contented with the privilege of being the loyal subjects of the Big White Chief in London.

The Fijian society is still tribal. Most of the leaders in the government were Chiefs of different tribes and their rank in society was largely governed by the rank and standing of their tribes. The Governor-General was the Chief of an important tribe. It was his direct ancestor who gifted away the island to the British. Ratu Mara, the Prime Minister, was himself head of a tribe, but his wife was head of another tribe, which in tribal hierarchy ranked above Ratu Mara's tribe. In Fijian society, she commanded a place of respect higher than that of the Prime Minister though in the official hierarchy he had the position of Prime Minister.

We witnessed an interesting demonstration of the acknowledgement of Mrs Ratu Mara's primacy at a function organised by the government in honour of Mrs Gandhi immediately after our arrival at Suva. We were driven straight from the airport to a ceremonial function of welcome at an open ground and we found a large number of tribal chieftains in various types of tribal dress or "undress" squatting on the ground wanting to pay homage to the visiting "chief" from India. The Prime Minister and her party and the Fijian Prime Minister, his wife and senior cabinet colleagues and other government dignitaries were seated on a high platform. The Chief of each tribe sang his welcome song or said his piece following the cue given by a master of ceremonies. The Chiefs had a demonstratively suppliant posture sitting on their knees with their forelegs bent under them. After reciting their salutations in their native dialects to the big Chief – this time the honour was for Indira Gandhi – they came upto the platform and placed their presents respectfully before her. The presents were a wide assortment of items – pigs, fruits, handicrafts, baskets, etc. After the ceremony of paying homage ended, the Chiefs started an elaborate ritual of making a concoction which was supposed to be Fijian wine from several roots, herbs and fibres. The main Chief squeezed the herbs and fibres into a wooden vessel while his followers kept singing and gesticulating. The whole process took a very long time, but we all had to wait patiently because none could ask the Chiefs to hurry up or dispense with any part of the established rituals and formalities. After a good deal of squeezing and mixing of several bunches of roots and herbs, the Chief poured the liquid into a small wooden cup and holding it with both hands approached Mrs Gandhi with great reverence and offered the cup to her. We were waiting to see what Mrs Gandhi would do with this concoction, but just as was expected from a "Big Chief", she emptied the cup in one drink without showing any sign of uneasiness or embarrassment. The entire crowd broke into loud applause at this gesture. The second person to be handed over the cup was Ratu Mara's wife and not Ratu Mara, in recognition of her senior rank in the tribal hierarchy. Ratu Mara was the third person to be offered this liquid and the turn of other Fijian VIPs followed in strict tribal hierarchical order with which they all were quite familiar. The members of the delegation also received their share of the concoction, which I remember, tasted like pungent vinegar.

The Fijians of Indian origin were very much the political have-nots in that country. Even though they constituted more than half the population of the Island, they had no effective share in the power structure. The Melanesian Fijians with the support of the Whites were in real control of the administration of the country. The Constitution had been so framed that only the group which had the support of the Whites could form the government. The Indian community was sharply divided into various religious and linguistic groups and there was no recognised leader for the community as a whole.

The Prime Minister's visit to the "Girmit" centre which is one of the important places connected with the history of Indian immigration to the Islands, was a major event for the entire community. 'Girmit' is the corrupted Fijian term for 'agreement' which referred to the contract between the indentured labourer from India and his employer. The Indian labourers who were brought to these Islands over a century ago, could under this agreement settle down on a piece of land allotted to them after completing the stipulated period of bonded labour. The oldest members of the community, about fifteen or twenty, were specially introduced to the Prime Minister. Some of them, in their eighties or even nineties, had come to the Island as little kids or were born there to the first generation immigrants and were very nostalgic about their Indian origins.

An old man in an advanced stage of senility caught hold of my hands and started reciting to me a prayer in Tamil. It never seemed to end and the old man would not let me go till he had come to the end of his prayer. It was a prayer in praise of Lord Muruga and he assured me that Lord Muruga has been protecting the Island and the Indian community from the dangers of evil people all these years.

For the Fijians of Indian origin, it was a great day of rejoicing. Most of them seemed to know Hindustani well. In fact, Hindustani was one of the important bonds of unity among them. The Prime Minister announced a donation of five lakh rupees to the "Girmit" centre. In the various speeches she made during the visit, she reminded the people of the need for total loyalty to the new country while being always proud of the land of their ancestors and their cultural heritage.

Tonga

Our next visit was to Tonga, an idyllic speck of an island in the Pacific with a population of a few thousand people ruled by a king of gigantic size but of very gentle manners and sophisticated tastes looking like some sort of a phantom from a fairy tale. The queen, a very cultured and gracious lady, was herself of unusually large size, but the king was a person really out of the ordinary. He spoke excellent English and was quite knowledgeable on world politics and particularly interested in ecology, forest conservation, etc. He had visited India on two occasions and had extended a warm invitation to Indira Gandhi to visit his kingdom. We were received at the airport by the Prime Minister and senior ministers, all of whom were brothers and cousins of the king. Indira Gandhi stayed at the king's palace, while the rest of the delegation stayed in a hotel, the only one of international standards in the country.

The most fascinating and memorable experience of this visit was the royal feast hosted by the king in honour of Indira Gandhi. The entire population of Tonga had turned up, the more important among them participating in the feast, sitting in the special enclosure along with the Indian guests, in the strict order of their rank in their society and the rest just watching the guests eat from outside the enclosure. The king, the queen, Indira Gandhi and two or three senior members of her delegation and some senior members of the royal establishment were on an elevated platform, but squatting on cushioned seats with back rests. We had a problem of adjusting our legs because we were neither sitting on chairs nor on the floor. We found the king and the queen very comfortable in this position in spite of their massive physical proportions. It was a noon meal - to call it a meal will be a gross understatement – and it lasted nearly two-and-a-half hours. In front of us, there was a one-foot high narrow table stretching from one end to the other and heaped on it were mountains of food of all varieties and sizes – whole pigs roasted, huge chunks of lamb, giant-sized lobsters, fish of all sizes, a wide assortment of fruits, vegetables and salads and huge quantities of cooked rice. The food placed in front of each one of us was enough to feed ten like us, but we were told that this was the king's hospitality for his honoured guests and we need not worry about the quantities wasted because what pleased the king was that we were there to partake of his meal. Squatting on their knees opposite each of us were pretty maids helping us to cut the meat or the fish and symbolically driving away flies with a broom of leaves. They kept waving the brooms, though no flies were visible and we were told that this was part of the ritual at the royal feasts.

I was sitting to the right of the queen and she kept explaining to me in very good English how some of the important dishes were prepared. She said that she herself was quite interested in cooking and had personally supervised the preparation of some of the main dishes for that day's feast, as she wanted to make sure that Indira Gandhi, for whom she had great respect, had an enjoyable meal. She was helping herself liberally to chunks of a particular dish and placed a few pieces on my plate recommending them to me as a very special delicacy. When I asked what it was, she said in all casualness that it was "octopus"! My appetite disappeared totally on knowing the name of the delicacy served specially by royal hands for my delight and I could not bring myself to eating any fish or meat at that meal thereafter. My only anxiety was that the queen should not ask me how I enjoyed the octopus as I would have had to utter a diplomatic lie to avoid discourtesy to my royal hostess.

The feast was followed by a folk dance in the open grounds nearby. Here again, the king and the guests were seated on a raised platform while other invitees were seated at a lower level. In Tonga, the king has to be seated always at an elevated place well above the level where his subjects are seated. A large number of Tongan men and women were doing a dance on the ground to the beat of drums. As the dance went on, some spectators came forward and gave currency notes to selected dancers in token of their appreciation of their performance. There was a solo dance item by a little child, the grand-daughter of the king and predictably a very large number of spectators came forward to express their appreciation by giving her gifts of money. For many Tongans, this was an excellent opportunity to show their loyalty to the king.

Indira Gandhi hosted a dinner in honour of the king on 28 September. According to the Tonga Custom, if the king visited any house other than that of his close relatives, that house became the property of the king. We had, therefore, to arrange the dinner at the house of the king's brother-in-law, which by tradition, would not become the king's property in spite of his visit there. Again by custom, the king and queen had to sit at a place higher than that of their subjects. Therefore, the king, the queen, Indira Gandhi, and some of the senior members of our delegation were seated around a table inside the house, while the Tongan invitees and other members of our delegation had their seats at a lower level on the verandah of the house. We had known from the experience of the king's previous visits to India that he was very fond of mutton pilau and chicken curry and we had made special arrangements for serving these favourite dishes of the king at this dinner. I was sitting next to the queen and watching with great interest how well the king was enjoying his meal. A double helping of pilau and chicken curry was served first on a thali to the king and in a matter of three or four minutes, he finished eating it. Very promptly, the bearer brought a new thali equally well laden and placed it before the king. By that time, we were only just beginning to start eating our first spoonful of pilau.

Throughout the dinner, the king kept up a very interesting conversation on environment protection, trees, forests, sea food, etc. I was quite impressed by the depth and range of his knowledge on these subjects. On the whole, I can say that the King of Tonga is one of the most interesting personalities I have come across in my life. Those who have met him once can never forget this affable personality of massive size, great wisdom, gentleness and gracious manners.

Australia

Indira Gandhi then visited Australia to attend the Commonwealth heads of government conference at Melbourne. The security arrangements at the hotel where most of the visiting delegations were accommodated and at the venue of the conference were the strictest I had so far seen. This time the Prime Minister had included Foreign Minister, P.V. Narasimha Rao as a member of her delegation. Each head of delegation was allowed to take only two aides inside the conference hall. P.V. Narasimha Rao and I were the two aides who attended the meeting along with Mrs Gandhi. The other members of the delegation, who had come to Melbourne in connection with the conference were in the lounge along with the members of other delegations.

Mrs Gandhi was never a passive spectator at any meeting. She closely followed every statement made at the conference and kept asking me for facts and figures and on our government's position on various points raised in their speeches. Attending a conference as an aide to Mrs Gandhi was a very demanding job. One had always to be alert and ready with answers to her various queries.

The first thing that I noticed while attending this conference was the special respect and deference which Indira Gandhi's Commonwealth colleagues showed her. She was one of the seniormost members of the Commonwealth club, having been Prime Minister from 1966 with a break of only three years during 1977-80. Even before becoming Prime Minister, she had accompanied her father to several of these conferences. Apart from any other consideration, the Prime Minister of a country which had a population more than that of all the other Commonwealth countries put together had a special position in that club. Everyone recognised the fact that the Commonwealth minus India would only be a shadow of its present existence. Mrs Gandhi was on intimate first-name terms with several Commonwealth leaders. Julius Nyerere was Julius to her. Kenneth Kaunda was Ken, and Pierre Trudeau was Pierre. In turn, they addressed her as Indira. Kenneth Kaunda made a very warm reference to Indira Gandhi's presence at Melbourne after she had missed the previous Commonwealth meeting at Lusaka: "We specially welcome you, Indira, to this meeting", he said "We all indeed missed you at Lusaka".

The Prime Minister hosted some lunches and dinners for small groups of her Commonwealth colleagues. I was a regular invitee to all official lunches and dinners hosted by the Prime Minister in India or when I was travelling with her abroad. These were highly valuable opportunities to make acquaintance with the "big ones" of the world and to talk to them on India's position on various issues or give them the correct facts about important developments in India. Above all, these were valuable opportunities for me to watch Mrs Gandhi at work in the delicate art of international diplomacy of which she was an unrivalled expert. These were also good occasions to listen to interesting stories and anecdotes of the "big ones".

At one of these dinner conversations at Melbourne, the subject turned to Idi Amin of Uganda. Most of the guests had some interesting anecdote to narrate about Idi Amin. Indira Gandhi also had one. While attending a conference of heads of Non-Aligned countries at Algiers, she received a special request from Idi Amin, who was also attending the same conference, for a meeting with her. She received him with courtesy but throughout the meeting she did not say anything except a few words of welcome on meeting and again of farewell at Amin's departure. But Amin was not the one to be put off by such signals. What was important for him was that he should have a meeting with Indira Gandhi even though it was all a one-sided talk. Idi Amin came to meet her accompanied by half-a-dozen Indians, including a couple of Sikhs, who were introduced to her as very senior officials of his government. But Mrs Gandhi had known in advance that Idi Amin had sent out his aides to collect a group of Indians from the city to accompany him on his visit to her to create the impression that his top aides were still Indians and the reports about his having driven out Indians from key positions in his government in Uganda were all false.

Indira Gandhi was the main centre of attention at the Commonwealth conference because of the fact of her spectacular return to power when everyone in the west had written her off. Wherever she went, there were pressing requests from ministers, senior officials and other dignitaries attending the conference for her autograph or autographed photograph. The Press Conference at Canberra arranged by the Australian Press Club and addressed by her was, according to our hosts, one of the largest ever held by this Club. Every seat was taken by members of the press who had paid 15 US dollars per seat. Mrs Gandhi was in her best form and handled the questions with superb skill. The Chairman, concluding the press conference thought that he was paying Mrs Gandhi a great compliment when he said: "Mrs. Gandhi, you are indeed a most remarkable woman". But the woman in her would not allow her to let that compliment pass as it was. She quickly got hold of the mike in front of her and said "I thank you for your kind words, but I would rather be referred to as a human being. I am not a feminist, but I don't think that a person should be referred to as a man or woman, but should be treated only as a person". There was a loud applause from the gathering and the loudest was from the women at the conference who appeared to be quite pleased by her statement.

The Philippines

Our next halt was Manila. Mrs Gandhi had decided to include Philippines in her visit to Australia, as the Marcoses had been pressing her for a visit, even for a day.

The Marcoses had indeed done their very best to make Mrs Gandhi's visit to their country a memorable one. From the time her plane touched down at the airport, till her departure the next day, it was flag waving and cheering crowds all the way and everywhere. Mrs Marcos had taken personal charge of the arrangements at all the functions. After the ceremonies, I was getting ready to go into the car allotted to me when Mrs Marcos came to me and insisted that I should ride with her in her car. "I have information that you were mainly responsible for making Mrs Gandhi accept our invitation and I want to thank you personally for this" she said with a girl-like candour.

The Marcoses hosted a glittering banquet in Mrs Gandhi's honour on 8 October. Mr and Mrs Marcos, Mrs Gandhi and I stood in line to be introduced to all the invitees before the start of the banquet. Mr Marcos in his speech almost exhausted his vocabulary of superlatives in praise of Mrs Gandhi. She in her reply had a special word of praise for the "charming and beautiful first lady", which the latter appreciated heartily. During the banquet, there were loud demands from the assembled Filippino guests that Mrs Marcos should sing and she had been pretending to be unwilling to concede to such a request. But all this was obviously a pre-arranged scenario where she would be seen to relent at the pressing request of her admirers and as a very special gesture to her distinguished guest. Imelda Marcos gave a wonderful display of her undoubtedly great talents in singing, by first giving a solo and later joining in a group song. We could see that the rich and resonant voice which had captured the heart of Marcos as a young man had not lost any of its power and impact in spite of her not having had regular practice.

On 9 October, Mrs Marcos hosted an all-ladies lunch in honour of Mrs Gandhi. There were over a thousand ladies at the lunch and about ten of us men accompanying the Prime Minister. It was a magnificent show of style, glitter and glamour. As we were having our lunch, an elaborate spectacle in which several hundreds of dancers, singers and various artistes participated was going on on the stage. For sheer splendour, it was a spectacular event executed with perfection. Outside the hall, thousands of school children, band players and dancers had been assembled to cheer Mrs Gandhi and bid her farewell.

Mrs Marcos then took Mrs Gandhi and some of us members of her party on a conducted tour of a few selected places in Manila. She herself acted as the guide, explaining through the loudspeaker the special features of various buildings and monuments and incidentally mentioning how some of the new building complexes, hospitals, etc., had been planned and executed under the personal supervision of the Governor of metropolitan Manila. An aide of Mrs Marcos did not fail to inform us over the microphone that that distinguished functionary was none other than Mrs Marcos herself. The farewell at the airport was again a grand show – huge cheering crowds, school children, bands and dances.

When we boarded the plane for our return journey, most of us were so fatigued and exhausted by the strain of the hectic visit to five countries that we slumped into our seats for a well-deserved

The author and Sharada Prasad getting a draft cleared from Indira Gandhi

The author with Indira Gandhi before the start of a press conference

Indira Gandhi addressing a press conference in Cyprus

Indira Gandhi sharing a joke with Mrs Alexander

Indira Gandhi planting a tree on the grounds of her old school in Switzerland

Mrs Gandhi holding discussions in Kuwait

**Indira Gandhi with the ruler of the
United Arab Emirates (U.A.E.)**

Indira Gandhi with Prime Minister Ratu Mara of Fiji

Indira Gandhi on arrival in Manila

Mrs Gandhi with President Reagan at the White House

Indira Gandhi in Moscow

Indira Gandhi in Athens with Melina Mercouri

Indira Gandhi talking to Julius Nyerere at the heads of governments meet at New York

Indira Gandhi in a meeting with M.G. Ramachandran in Madras

Last photograph of Indira Gandhi, taken at Bhubaneswar on 30 October 1984

sleep and rest. But not so Indira Gandhi. Within minutes of the take-off she called for the file boxes received from Delhi and spent the entire time of the return journey on the plane clearing these. For her, there was no time to lose, because more files and work were awaiting her arrival at Delhi and she wanted to dispose of all the files she had received from Delhi in the meanwhile. My rest and sleep had to be interrupted as I was being called into her cabin off and on for discussions on some issue or other relating to those files. In the course of time, I was to get used to this hectic pace of working with a person who never tired.

Romania, Mexico, U.K. : 18-27 October 1981

Within nine days of our return from the hectic tour in five countries of South-East Asia and Australia, we were again on the move. The main purpose of the tour this time was to attend the heads of government meeting at Cancun, Mexico. L.K. Jha and G. Parthasarathi, who were members of our delegation to Cancun had gone there in advance along with the senior officials from the ministry of External Affairs. The delegation to Romania included Mrs Sonia Gandhi, who as usual kept a very low profile.

Our first halt was at Bucharest, Romania. President Ceausescu himself was present at the airport to receive Indira Gandhi – an honour reserved by him for only very special visitors. Mrs Gandhi had a fairly long one-to-one meeting with the President, while I led the Indian delegation for talks with the Romanian ministers and senior officials on bilateral trade and economic co-operation. The Romanian economy was in poor shape with problems of heavy indebtedness and high cost of production. In the early years of Indo-Romanian economic co-operation, India used to buy a wide range of machine tools and equipment from that country. But we were now not only producing such goods ourselves, but were even exporting some of them. The Romanians were keen to sell us steel plants, power generating units, drilling equipment and what not, but we could not do much business with them as we found that neither their technology nor their price was good enough for us. The talks, however, were held in a very cordial atmosphere and we decided to continue the exercise of identifying items which could be of interest to both sides. One serious problem in promoting trade and economic co-operation with Romania was that we had in Delhi a

Romanian Ambassador who believed that Romania was a super industrial power and that India should go all out to grasp its hand of co-operation which it was kind enough to extend to us. The Ambassador believed that Romania could supply India anything it needed and lead us on the path of industrial progress. Modesty was not his strong point and, therefore, he did not care to know the opinion which people outside his country had about Romania's industrial strength.

We left Bucharest on the morning of 20 October for Cancun. We broke journey at Montreal for a night's rest and reached Cancun at 10 a.m. on 21 October.

The Cancun Summit

The idea of a conference of twenty-two heads of government representing North and South and East and West to seek solutions for the great issues relating to peace and development had roused considerable interest and expectation all over the world. Many believed that Cancun would come up with solutions which had eluded the UN so far and that the informal format designed for this summit would help cut through the intractable mess which months of marathon debates in the UN and other forums had thrown these problems into. The fact that the conference was to be attended by the heads of governments of U.S.A., U.K., France and China and by eminent leaders of the Third World like the Presidents of Mexico and Tanzania and the Prime Minister of India had given it a special importance and it was slated to be the boldest attempt at summitry aimed at breaking the deadlock that had developed in the North South dialogue.

It looked as if the big bosses of the world had grown impatient at the manner in which their diplomats at the UN were handling these life and death issues of peace and development and had decided to take these issues into their own hands and deal with them themselves in an effort to save humanity from the disaster to which it was plunging headlong. But within a few hours of the start of the conference, it became clear to us that Cancun was going to be just another conference ending in a highly diluted consensus declaration leading to nowhere, one more non-event in the chequered history of North-South dialogue. At the conference, we were to hear the same familiar arguments which had already been advocated by the

Northern countries at the UN on every issue discussed. The only difference was that this time we were having them straight from the horse's mouth and not through diplomats at new York or Geneva.

All delegates to the conference were put up in the same hotel at Cancun and the meeting itself was at the conference room of the hotel. This was done to save time, and also the trouble involved in arranging security for the movement of the VIPs. The conference room on the ground floor of the hotel had an oval table. The Prime Minister of Canada and the President of Mexico, the two chairmen of the conference, sat at the middle of the table while other heads of government were seated round the table in alphabetical order of the names of their countries. The central place of the room covered by the table was filled with flowers, mostly chrysanthemums. Each head of government had one member of his delegation to sit by his side at the table and two to sit behind. In the case of India, L.K. Jha occupied the chair next to the Prime Minister's while G. Parthasarathi and I sat immediately behind her. At the back of this room, about a hundred yards away, was the roaring ocean. The conference room had glass walls on all sides, but security men saw to it that no unwanted person came anywhere near the room. There was a large lounge near the conference room where coffee and snacks were available. Those entering the conference room had to wear special badges for identification, but there was an indisciplined crowd of pressmen and TV crew and photographers at the entrance to the conference room, which made a mockery of all security arrangements. As each VIP arrived or departed, there was a mad rush of pressmen at him and quite a bit of pushing and wrestling by the Mexican security guards and the VIP's personal security guards.

On the 21st afternoon, Indira Gandhi had her first meeting with President Reagan in his hotel suite. She was accompanied by L.K. Jha, G. Parthasarathi and me. The American security men had installed an electronic screening door on the corridor about thirty yards from the entrance to the President's suite. None could reach the President's room except through this screening door. We all went through this door and were duly escorted to a room where Secretary of State Alexander Haig, Secretary to the Treasury, Donald Regan and Security Adviser Allen received us. They were wearing casual shirts or bush shirts, and there was an air of informality in the room. We were shown to our seats on one side of the table, while the U.S. officials sat on the other. We were told that President Reagan would join us in a couple of minutes. The Chinese Prime Minister was with the President at that time and he was expected to leave very soon. The President came to the room in two minutes and shook hands with each of us. He was wearing a light brown sports shirt and the atmosphere in the room, at least as far as the Americans in sports shirts were concerned, was more like a picnic than a meeting of two heads of government who were meeting each other for the first time.

Mrs Gandhi had indicated her preference for a one-to-one meeting with Reagan, while we were to carry on our talks with Alexander Haig and his Party and the Americans had agreed to this. Reagan and Mrs Gandhi, therefore, went to the terrace adjacent to our room, but a large crowd of TV and cameramen had already taken position on the terrace and what was intended to be a quiet tete-a-tete turned out to be a prolonged photo-session cutting into the time available for the talk between the two VIPs. After the photographers were dismissed, the two started talking, but within a few minutes a drizzle started and they both had to join us in our room.

Mrs Gandhi later told us that they could not discuss any subject fully or seriously. Her idea of a one-to-one meeting was to establish a personal rapport with the man. This had been her style of diplomacy which had proved remarkably successful in many cases. Sometimes, such meetings intended for half-an-hour had gone on for one or even one-and-a-half hour at a stretch. It was her practice to tell us the gist of the talks to enable us to record a short note of the matters discussed. But what was really more important about such meetings was the friendship and understanding that could be established between two human beings which were later to be developed by further such contacts. Judged from this objective, this meeting was a complete failure. Mrs Gandhi told me later that it should be taken as a non-event as she could not get Reagan to talk seriously on any personal or official matter. Probably Reagan was not prepared for this type of meeting, particularly with a person whom he was meeting for the first time and with whom he had serious differences of opinion on many matters. She said that Reagan had been uncomfortable from the beginning of the meeting and the drizzle came as a welcome excuse for him to join us in the room.

While the Prime Minister and the President were meeting at the terrace, we were exchanging views on some issues of serious concern to both the countries. Alexander Haig who was conducting the talks, came straight to the question of American supply of arms to Pakistan, a subject which he knew was uppermost in our minds. The Americans came out with their oft-repeated argument that American arms were intended to strengthen Pakistan to meet the Soviet threat. L.K. Jha asked me to state the Indian position on this. I said that Pakistan did not appear to really believe that it needed Americans arms to fight the Soviets. I told the Americans that we had reliable information that the Pakistanis had assured the Soviets that they did not entertain any fear of an attack from them. This assurance was repeated a few weeks earlier when the Soviet Deputy Foreign Minister visited Pakistan. If the Pakistanis did not perceive any threat from the Soviets, I said, they did not need any weapons to use against them. I said that the weapons were obviously intended only for use against us and we in turn were being forced to go in for more weapons to defend our territory. This resulted in diversion of scarce resources from development to defence and this was hurting us badly.

At this point, Mrs Gandhi and Reagan joined us from their terrace talks. Haig took the initiative for keeping up the dialogue and said, "Mr. President, you would like to exchange views with the Prime Minister on the agenda for tomorrow's meeting". We were expecting some very important comment or observation from the President on the Cancun agenda, but all that the President said was that a discussion on the agenda would indeed be useful. Realising that the President was not taking the cue, Haig prodded him further to say something on one item on the agenda which was of special importance to all developing countries, viz., food security. Again Reagan's reply was just a bland statement that food security was indeed a very important issue. I got the clear impression that he was not very knowledgeable on the issues for discussion at the summit and was not even seriously interested in knowing what the views of the developing countries were on these vital matters of concern to them. I immediately realised that his attendance at the summit was going to be just in the nature of a ritualistic concession to public opinion and not a serious attempt at seeking solutions to the grave problems facing the developing countries. Reagan had a vacant look and an undisguised expression of boredom for what was going on in the room.

Mrs Gandhi tried to keep the talk on food security going by explaining how several developing countries were still struggling with the basic problem of food and how they found it difficult to cope with the periodic recurrence of droughts, floods, etc. Haig tried to interest the President in India's success in agricultural production in recent years. "India's experience should prove to be useful to other developing countries," he said and turning to the President, added: "Mr. President, you would like to know from the Prime Minister how India was able to achieve this success". The President merely repeated this statement to Mrs Gandhi and she then gave a brief account of the strategy India had followed in achieving her Green Revolution. At the end of her intervention she turned to me and said, "Alexander, would you like to add to what I have said"? I supplemented her statement by explaining the arrangements for liberal agricultural credit to farmers and for agricultural extension service through the network of extension experts. The subject of agricultural production apparently caught Reagan's interest, but he used the opportunity only to tell us about the virtues of private enterprise which we were to hear on several occasions later too in the course of our stay in Cancun. He told us how private enterprise had succeeded in bringing about the agricultural revolution in his country and how because of the efficiency of its private enterprise, U.S. was not only able to feed its own people but also several millions in other countries who were dependent on US food exports. I could see the cynical smile on Mrs Gandhi's face but she did not want to enter into any argument with President Reagan on these issues. He was entitled to his own views on the role of private enterprise and it was not Mrs Gandhi's habit to indulge in arguments on theoretical or ideological issues with other people.

The meeting between the heads of the two largest democracies of the world soon ended with a few more such general comments by President Reagan. Mrs Gandhi had already become disillusioned about the whole meeting. She had hoped that it would throw up something useful for further discussions, but it ended up as a mere exercise in courtesy – a display of diplomatic politeness without a meeting of the minds. Mrs Gandhi told me later that day that she was quite disappointed about the man and his lack of grasp of the issues before the conference and that in these circumstances she did not expect that anything important would emerge from the Cancun summit.

On the question of the virtues of private enterprise and its relevance to developing countries, President Reagan was to listen to some plain speaking the next day at the main conference from President Julius Nyerere of Tanzania. The provocation came when Reagan repeated his piece on the role of private enterprise in economic development and asked Third World countries to avail themselves of the experience and expertise of private enterprise from developed countries in their development efforts. Unlike Mrs Gandhi, Julius Nyerere was not overburdened by diplomatic niceties on such occasions. On the contrary, Nyerere was always very blunt and direct and did not bother to couch his views in diplomatic language or in understatements. Addressing President Reagan directly, he said: "Mr. President, tell me which private entrepreneur from developed countries is interested in building roads or canals in developing countries? There is no money in such projects and, therefore, they are of no interest to them. What can private enterprise from your countries do to help agricultural production in our countries when there are no roads or railways to transport their produce?" President Nyerere's language was forthright and his manner and his style of talking compelled the attention of the listeners, though they might not quite like them. President Reagan was, of course, not too pleased at having to listen to a blunt refutation of his thesis on private enterprise.

Listening to President Reagan at our bilateral meeting and later watching his performance at the conference, the feeling I had was one of deep disillusionment. I expected to see in the President, elevated to the highest position in his country by a very elaborate process of election, an alert and well-informed person with genuine involvement in the issues under discussion and a great degree of comprehension. I was probably expecting too much from the American system of election and thinking that American democracy can always pick out the best man for the top position of power. Those were the early years of Reagan Administration and the world had not yet grown disillusioned about his personal abilities, which had a larger-than-life media build-up during the election campaign. Perhaps I had expected too much from the

American President and, therefore, I felt more disappointed at this first experience of meeting him.

Attending such conferences with Indira Gandhi was no relaxation for someone like me. One had always to be on one's toes and burdened with the responsibility of ensuring that everything went off smoothly. One had to be present at every important meeting, formal or informal, which the Prime Minister attended, and be ready with facts and figures and the latest information. I remember how totally exhausted I was by the end of the second day. I had returned to my room in the hotel at about 7.30 p.m. and had just stretched myself on the bed hoping to be ready and relaxed for a dinner I was to attend along with the Prime Minister an hour later. When I woke up, I found it was 2.00 a.m. and I had been sleeping with my trousers, tie and socks on! The strain of work in Cancun truly really left me exhausted.

The Cancun conference, hailed as one of the boldest attempts at breaking the North-South stalemate, ended as an anticlimax with a lot of wasted words and empty rhetoric. The world was none the better or worse for it.

London

We left Cancun on the evening of 25 October and reached London on the 26th morning on our way back home.

Our halt at London was mainly a refuelling one and to break the long journey from Mexico to Delhi. The Prime Minister stayed in the Indian High Commissioner's house at Kensington Palace Gardens while the rest of the delegation stayed in city hotels.

Dr. Syed Mohammed, the High Commissioner, had been feeling quite uncomfortable in his job ever since he got into trouble with some influential Indian residents in England. They had managed to create in the Prime Minister the impression that Syed Mohammed was unequal to his job and that his continuance in this post would not be conducive to promotion of goodwill for India in UK. A distinguished person who had earned his law degree and doctorate in law from London, Dr. Syed Mohammed had held several high positions in India with great distinction. He was Advocate-General in Kerala and Minister of State for Law in the Union Council of Ministers. The post of High Commissioner, to which he had been appointed by Mrs Gandhi was in no way an undeserved position of honour for him. Dr. Syed Mohammed knew about the campaign that had been mounted against him and was greatly worried that several baseless rumours had been floated against him to tarnish his fair name and image. There were rumours of his transfer to another Mission and he felt that a transfer from London before the expiry of the normal term of a High Commissioner would be a humiliation for him at this stage of his life. He poured his heart out to me and I in turn told him to keep his cool and equanimity. I assured him that Mrs Gandhi would come to know the correct facts about the allegations against him and he should have confidence in her doing what was fair and just. Eventually, Syed Mohammed not only completed his full term in London, but got a year and a half's extension to boot and returned to India earning Mrs Gandhi's appreciation for the good work he had done in connection with the Festival of India.

Indira Gandhi had no official business in London, apart from holding discussions with the High Commissioner. However, as usual, she was not wasting her time in 9 Kensington Palace Gardens. She found the house – one of the most magnificent buildings in this area generally known as the Millionaires' Row – in a rather shabby shape. The curtains were showing their age, the furniture covers had visible stains of long use, the furniture in several rooms needed repair, the floor coverings were faded and worn out and on the whole she found the house in very poor condition. Syed Mohammed told the Prime Minister that he had been repeatedly asking for funds for replacement of the old drapery and furniture, but the ministry had not bothered to consider his requests. Mrs Gandhi took the trouble to visit every room and note down personally the changes and replacements required. She even had the furniture in the main living rooms re-arranged to give them a more presentable appearance. Within a few days of her return to Delhi, the funds asked for earlier by the High Commissioner were sanctioned by the ministry. What was more, the ministry sanctioned additional funds for the urgently needed facelift for the house on the lines indicated by Mrs Gandhi. She had always a keen eye for tidiness and elegance and 9 Kesington Palace Gardens, of which I became the occupant four years later, indeed benefited a good deal by her brief stay there.

On the 27th night, G. Parthasarathi and I went to see the famous play *Evita*. We were half through the play when we received the message that the Prime Minister had decided to advance the time of departure from London by four hours and we had, therefore, to rush to the airport to join the rest of the delegation. We were back in Delhi on the 28th morning, back to the familiar scene at the airport – garlands, bouquets, press conference – to more work and to clearance of arrears which had accumulated during an absence of nine days.

There were no more foreign travels in 1981 but eleven countries in six months were a handful indeed.

1982

United Kingdom : 21–27 March 1982

The main purpose of Mrs Gandhi's visit to the United Kingdom in 1982 was to inaugurate the Festival of India which had been organised with great care and attention by a team of experts under the leadership of Pupul Jayakar. The Festival, which was to last several months, was intended to present to the people of the UK a representative sample of India's ancient cultural heritage and also her achievements in the field of science and technology. Performances by leading exponents of various forms of classical and folk music and dance and exhibition of priceless treasures of Indian art from different museums and private collections had been included in the Festival programmes. A good number pieces of Indian art were already with museums and private collectors in the U.K.and some of them were being exhibited along with those taken from India. This was the first of the Indian Festivals organised abroad and was soon to become the model for several other festivals to follow. Indira Gandhi had taken personal interest in the planning of the Festival and had provided advice and expert guidance at every stage of its organisation. The Festival was expected to generate its inevitable spin-off in improved trade, tourism and economic relations but the focus was on the art and culture of India of which there was quite a lot of ignorance in the U.K. in spite of a couple of hundred years of colonial link. A whole generation had grown up in the U.K. after India's independence which knew little of India, and the Festival was intended to bring to their doors a bit of India and to stimulate in them an interest in India. There were several bilateral economic issues for discussion and the Prime Minister's visit provided a good opportunity for such discussions as well.

We landed at the Heathrow airport, London, at 6.30 p.m. on 21 March. Prime Minister Margaret Thatcher had come to the airport to welcome Indira Gandhi. We had received reports that some Sikhs had planned to stage a black flag demonstration on Mrs Gandhi arrival. We did not see any such demonstration at the airport. On the other hand, there was a large gathering of Indians including several Sikhs, at the airport to receive Mrs Gandhi and they gave her a tremendous ovation. As we were moving out of the airport area we saw a small group of about 30-40 Sikhs with black flags and placards. The British police had kept the small group of demonstrators at an inconspicuous place.

Our first official programme in London was a meeting with Mrs Thatcher and her colleagues at her official residence. We reached No.10 Downing Street at 11 a.m. and the two Prime Ministers met separately without aides for an hour while the official level talks were held in an adjacent room. The Indian team for the talks was led by me and the UK team by Douglas Hurd, then minister of State for Foreign Affairs. We were then called into the room where the two Prime Ministers were having their meeting and asked to report the gist of our talks. Mrs Thatcher was in a charmingly informal mood and she appeared to be keen to accommodate our requests and suggestions on bilateral economic co-operation. Mrs Thatcher had met Mrs Gandhi on two or three earlier occasions and the two leaders had developed great respect and liking for each other. Both were extremely forceful and influential persons within their respective parties and countries and both shared the great quality of courage in decision making. Mrs Thatcher knew that her counterpart, leading the government of a much larger and more difficult and complex country, had far more serious problems to handle than she had and this had only enhanced her admiration for her. Mrs Thatcher told me on several occasions during my assignment in the U.K. later as Indian High Commissioner how much she had admired Mrs Indira Gandhi. This affection and respect which they had for each other were born out of a perfect understanding of each other acquired during the intimate talks they had together; their meeting in London was one such great opportunity.

I had met Mrs Thatcher at Melbourne and Cancun and, therefore, I was not a stranger to her. After listening to Douglas Hurd's account about our talks, Mrs Thatcher asked me to state the main points for further consideration. I invited special attention to the restrictions that had been imposed on exports of handloom products from India and explained the great hardship experienced by thousands of poor handloom weavers in India on account of these trade barriers. Another sensitive issue at that time was the proposed cut in the contribution to the International Development Assistance (IDA) Fund by the United States. The EEC countries had taken the stand that if the United States reduced its contribution they would cut their contributions proportionately. I pleaded that the EEC countries should put pressure on U.S.A. not to cut its contribution and that even if U.S.A. did not agree to this, U.K. should increase its contribution and thereby set an example to other countries who were insisting on the principle of proportionality vis-a-vis U.S.A.

Mrs Gandhi did not intervene in any of these issues except for making a few occasional comments. On matters concerning bilateral aid, Indira Gandhi had always been reluctant to appear as a supplicant for assistance before anyone. She had no hesitation to talk about multilateral aid, and whenever she intervened, it was on this subject and particularly to point out how IDA was crucial for some of the very poor developing countries of Africa. While asking for increased IDA we were not merely pressing our own case, but speaking on behalf of all developing countries receiving IDA, particularly African countries.

Mrs Thatcher's response was very helpful and positive. She argued with her own ministers and senior officials in our presence about the need for increased assistance to India and finally said that she would review the decision earlier taken by her government about the question of proportionality in IDA contributions.

The formal opening of the Festival by the Prince of Wales was a gala function attended by several distinguished men and women in the fields of administration, art and culture in the U.K. The two Prime Ministers and the Prince of Wales and other guests were treated to a splendid musical performance by M.S. Subbulakshmi. Pandit Ravi Shankar's sitar recital to the accompaniment of the London Philharmonia conducted by Zubin Mehta was another memorable event of the day.

Other events connected with the Festival and attended by Indira Gandhi included the inauguration of the Indian Science Exhibition by Mrs Thatcher and the Indian Sales Centre organised by Selfridges. As Mrs Gandhi entered the Selfridges stores on Oxford Street, we noticed that a large crowd of shoppers and shop assistants had gathered on the ground floor to see her. They cheered her wildly on seeing her at close quarters. I was quite amused to hear a middle-aged and rather heavy shop assistant at Selfridges, screaming loudly within the hearing of Mrs Gandhi herself: ''She is so pretty. She is so small''. Probably, she expected Indira Gandhi to be a huge and imposing personality like Golda Meir and was genuinely surprised to see Indira Gandhi looking many years younger than her age and dashing out of her car with the agility of a schoolgirl.

After the inauguration of the Science Exhibition by Mrs Thatcher, the two Prime Ministers were taken around to see the main exhibits. While going round the various rooms, Mrs Thatcher took me aside and told me that a decision had been taken by her earlier in the afternoon to increase U.K.'s contribution to IDA and also to increase U.K.'s bilateral aid to India from £ 75 million to £ 105 million and that I might convey this information to Indira Gandhi. I mentioned this to Mrs Gandhi at the exhibition itself and she was no doubt quite pleased at this most welcome and prompt result of her talks.

Indira Gandhi's programme in London was as usual an extremely crowded one, with every minute devoted to some meeting or visit. There was a meeting with a group of editors, interviews for the TV and the press, discussions with writers and intellectuals and meetings with leaders of the Indian community. In the midst of all these engagements, she found time to spend an hour at a centre for the rehabilitation of young spastic patients and to talk to some of the children and the doctors and nursing aides there.

The Prime Minister returned to Delhi on 27 March and at the press conference at the airport she was asked about her reaction to the reports that her daughter-in-law Maneka Gandhi was planning to attend the conference of some party dissidents at Lucknow the next day. She replied in a firm voice that any such conference would be an anti-party activity. She clearly intended this as a warning to Maneka that she should desist from such activities. But

Maneka, as subsequent events revealed, was not going to be deterred from going ahead with what she had already decided to do.

Saudi Arabia : 17-20 April 1982

Indira Gandhi's three-day visit to Saudi Arabia was politically far more important than her earlier visits to the other Islamic countries of the Gulf region. Saudi Arabia by tradition and history, was more Islamic than other Gulf countries and was also well known as a male bastion. The ruler King Khalid was in poor health and the prospects of having a meaningful talk with him were rather limited. However, the visit to Saudi Arabia had become important for India as Pakistan had been carrying on an open propaganda in that country against India's so-called anti-Islamic policies and alleged discrimination against its Muslim population. We had received reports that the propaganda had been fairly effective in certain high ruling circles and their attitude towards India was becoming rather unfriendly. The communal riots involving Hindus and Muslims in some parts of India had received exaggerated coverage in the Saudi media and the Pakistani propagandists were quick to present such unfortunate incidents as examples of the Indian government's indifference in providing security and protection to its Muslim citizens.

Pakistan, of course, had little to worry about Hindu-Muslim conflicts as the country had been practically swept clean of its Hindu population. The treatment which the Muslim minority groups such as the Shias and the Ahmedias had been getting in Pakistan was seldom allowed to appear in its true form in her own press because of the tight control which her military rulers exercised over it. Pakistan had also been carrying on a propaganda in Saudi Arabia about India's so-called sinister designs to further disintegrate and weaken that country and had been presenting India as a big bully trying to use every opportunity to keep Pakistan divided and weak. Of course, this type of anti-India propaganda suited Pakistan's designs which was a recipient of substantial aid from Saudi Arabia both for its defence and development programmes. The large presence of Pakistani military personnel in Saudi Arabia and of Pakistani civilians and experts in several crucial government departments and educational institutions helped Pakistan carry its anti-India propaganda to the right places. India had done very little to counter this propaganda. Even ministerial level meetings and exchanges of high level delegations had been very few and India's image by and large continued to remain distorted in that country. One of the important objectives of Indira Gandhi's visit to Saudi Arabia was to present to its leaders a correct picture of India as a truly secular State which made no distinction between its citizens on grounds of religion or creed and which entertained no desire to see Pakistan or any of its other neighbours weakened. There had also been a persistent propaganda that India was leaning more and more towards Soviet Russia's side and was soft on communism. India's commitment to socialistic principles were represented as pseudo-communism in this traditionally anti-communist country. And here again, India had not made any serious attempt to explain its true political and economic philosophy to the Saudi rulers. Indira Gandhi was aware of the important position which Saudi Arabia occupied in the Arab world and was keen to have an opportunity to present to its rulers the correct facts about the position of minorities in India and India's attitude to its neighbours and to the big powers.

Indira Gandhi was conscious of the fact that she was visiting an exclusive male corner of the world and had made discreet enquiries about the customs and practices followed by other women leaders during their visits to Saudi Arabia. Margaret Thatcher had visited Saudi Arabia a few weeks earlier and she had worn full sleeve dresses while in that country in deference to Saudi customs. Indira Gandhi wanted to be respectful to Saudi sentiments on women's dress to the extent possible and took care to wear full sleeve blouses during her meetings with the king and at the State banquets. She generally covered her head with her saree while in India, as was the custom for women in her home State Uttar Pradesh, and therefore, in this respect her style of dress in Saudi Arabia was the normal one she was used to while at home.

The Prime Minister's plane landed at Jeddah at 1230 hours on 17 April. The party included Pranab Mukherjee, Finance Minister, Khurshid Alam Khan, Minister of State for Tourism and Civil Aviation and Jaffer Shareef, Minister of State for Railways, besides me and a group of senior officials. Rajiv Gandhi arrived a day later to join the party. The formal State visit was to commence with the Prime Minister's arrival at Riyadh, the capital, the next day. At Jeddah the main function was laying the foundation stone of an

Indian school. A very large number of Indians had turned up at the place and we were indeed quite surprised to see such a big gathering of Indians in this Islamic city. Many of them were occupying high positions in medical and academic professions and seemed to have adjusted themselves happily to their new environment. The picture of Jeddah, as we saw it from the plane and drove through it, was that of a permanent construction site. It was full of high-rise buildings, many completed and many in varying stages of construction. At lunch we had the opportunity of meeting several prominent Saudi businessmen who were already doing fairly good business with India and who were keen to expand their business further.

The Prime Minister and party arrived at Riyadh from Jeddah to a very warm reception extended on behalf of the king by Crown Prince Fahd and senior members of the cabinet. We were all put up in the Conference Palace, a modern building – but constructed in the lavish Saudi style. The rooms were very large and richly decorated and those allotted to the Prime Minister and the senior members of the party were really very luxurious. The walls and floors were of marble and the carpets and the chandeliers were of exquisite quality. In this desert capital, our rooms and corridors had a liberal supply of fresh flowers flown in from Europe.

Indira Gandhi was shown utmost respect and deference by the Crown Prince and the senior cabinet ministers when they called on her in her suite. She met the senior ministers individually and explained to them India's position on major political issues and particularly on our policies towards Pakistan. Pranab Mukherji and I assisted her in these talks. Some of the ministers appeared somewhat shy and reserved to begin with, perhaps because they were not quite used to meeting a woman Prime Minister. But Indira Gandhi put them at ease in a few minutes by her informality. Among the senior ministers, prince Saud, the youthful Foreign Minister and Sheikh Yamani, the Minister of Petroleum, impressed Indira Gandhi as quite bright and knowledgeable in their subjects.

On the 19th evening King Khalid hosted a grand banquet in honour of Indira Gandhi. Before the banquet started the King received Indira Gandhi, Rajiv, the ministers accompanying the Prime Minister and me for talks. All the senior Princes – Fahd, Abdulla, Sultan, Saud – and all other senior ministers were present at this meeting. King Khalid appeared very ill and not very closely following the subjects we were talking about. He was being closely assisted by the Crown Prince and other senior princes. Indira Gandhi was trying her best to get the King interested in an intelligent discussion on Indo-Pakistan relations and on South-South co-operation in economic matters. But it was very difficult to carry on a meaningful conversation with the King in a fairly large group like that. When we adjourned for the banquet, Indira Gandhi could talk at length on these subjects to the King who was sitting by her side. The conversation, of course, was through an interpreter.

The banquet was indeed a lavish affair typical of the proverbial hospitality of the Saudi family. The senior Princes and ministers were at the head table along with the King and the Prime Minister and the senior members of her party. Indira Gandhi was the only woman at this banquet with over 300 guests. I was told that women are not normally invited to the King's banquet.

While at Riyadh, we were taken to see a racing event. There was no public or open betting on the horses. The invitees to the race were all members of the Saudi royal family and senior government officials. In honour of the Prime Minister's visit an Indira Gandhi prize was awarded to the winner of the race.

We left Riyadh for Daman on 20 April and after visiting the country's prestigious petroleum institute there, we left for Delhi in the afternoon. Crown Prince Fahd who had come to escort the Prime Minister from the Conference Palace to the airport at Riyadh had an hour's talk with her alone. Within a couple of days of Indira Gandhi's arrival in this country, she could establish an easy rapport with the Crown Prince and other Saudi ministers and create an atmosphere of cordiality and confidence. To begin with, there was some stiffness and formality, but very soon the talks became quite warm and informal as if they were meeting as old friends.

The visit to Saudi Arabia left a special impression on me. The desert atmosphere, rows and rows of skyscrapers, the continuous and everpresent construction activity, the visible dominance of Arab culture in the midst of the most modern comforts of living, and above all, the all-pervading impact of monarchical traditions captures one's attention immediately on one's arrival there. Even though I had visited some of the Gulf countries earlier, Saudi Arabia appeared to me different and unique. Perhaps, Mecca which dominates the whole atmosphere here gives this country its uniqueness. The royal family is the only institution that counts in this country. The government, the army, the social and economic activities are completely dominated by the family. The Saudi society with the royal family at the centre moves in several concentric circles within their appointed orbits and carefully determined distances measured by the degree of relationship to the centre. The affluence of the country strikes you straight in the eye. Plants and trees are maintained at extremely prohibitive costs to create the image of greenery in this desert land. Cost does not appear to figure in their economics and one gets the impression that one has stepped into a world with its own economic laws. Yet, there is the unfailing oriental courtesy and charm and a total absence of arrogance or upstartism in the midst of this mind-boggling affluence.

U.S.A. : 27 July-5 August 1982

A visit by an Indian Prime Minister to the U.S.A. is important in itself, but the present visit by Indira Gandhi was specially important, as it was her first to the U.S.A. after her return to power.

Mrs Gandhi was not particularly popular with the U.S. media; nor had she any close personal friend in the Regan administration. Her earlier visit to the U.S.A. and meetings with President Nixon on the eve of the Bangladesh war had won for her more enemies than friends in the American ruling circles as she had then stubbornly refused to be pressurised by the President and his advisers. The humiliating defeat of Pakistan in the Bangladesh war and the angry reaction of Nixon in sending the Seventh Fleet to the Indian Ocean to intimidate India had embittered Indo-U.S. relations and convinced Indira Gandhi that the American zeal for defence of democracy stopped at their own national frontiers. She used to say with bitter sarcasm that the world's greatest democracy was the world's greatest patron of dictators elsewhere and America even seemed to believe that support for dictators outside was necessary for preserving democracy in U.S.A. The U.S. media had invariably caricatured Indira Gandhi as an aggressive personality out to intimidate her weak neighbours. The Emergency rule of 1975-77 provided ample scope to the Indira-baiters in the U.S.A. to depict her as a power-hungry woman and the press had taken great delight in placing all the blame for some of the excesses of that period on her. The Janata government, whose main preoccupation was to destroy the political standing of Indira Gandhi, had used every means in its power to denigrate her in the foreign media as a subverter of democracy and the U.S. press had mercilessly gone at her during the years she was out of power. It was only after the bunglings and mismanagement of the Janata government that the western media began to reassess Indira Gandhi's role in running the government in a highly complex subcontinent like India. Even then most of the western media could not easily condone her bold stand on non-alignment or the frank manner in which she had raised her voice against the condescension and double standards of some of the western leaders towards developing countries. To most of them Indira Gandhi was an arrogant person, someone who had to be kept in her place by the continuous pressure of criticism.

The Treaty of Friendship and Co-operation which India had concluded with the Soviet Union in 1971 was in the eyes of the U.S. administration and media a confirmation of India's position as a Soviet client and many were inclined to write off India as a Soviet satellite. Even though the U.S. administration and media had moved very far from the Dullesian rigidity of the early 1950s, there was still no genuine understanding of the motives and sentiments behind India's commitment to non-alignment. To them, non-alignment was some form of expression of opposition to the U.S. and support for the Soviets. Indira Gandhi knew exactly where she stood in the assessment of the U.S. administration and, therefore, when she received the invitation to visit the U.S.A. she had genuine doubts whether the visit would prove to be useful or become counter-productive. She had serious misgivings that the American administration might persist in seeing her in the caricatured image of Soviet client they had drawn of her. Nevertheless, she had the confidence that she would be able to reach the American people directly. She believed that there was much in common between the American and Indian people and that whatever might be the attitude of those in the administration, she would be able to establish a good rapport with the American people for whom she had great admiration.

Indira Gandhi was keen to present to the American people a true image of democratic India and believed that the opportunities for speaking to the people directly would help a great deal in enabling them to appreciate India's policy of non-alignment. Her only doubt was whether the strong prejudices which the U.S. administration and media had developed against her as a person over a decade would inhibit this correct understanding of India's policies. She expressed such doubts several times to me whenever I discussed the details of the programme of the visit but behind all these doubts she had faith in the commitment of the average American to the basic values of democracy and to friendship for India as a democracy.

Indira Gandhi left for New York on 27 July. Her party included Rajiv and Sonia Gandhi, their children Rahul and Priyanka, G. Parthasarathi and me. Rasgotra, Foreign Secretary, Natwar Singh, Special Secretary, ministry of External Affairs and Arjun Sengupta, Additional Secretary, Prime Minister's Office had gone to Washington for pre-visit discussions with the U.S. officials a week in advance. We had a halt at Heathrow airport, London, for an hour and a half for refuelling; otherwise it was a non-stop flight from Delhi to New York. We were met at the London airport by Syed Mohammad, the Indian High Commissioner, Douglas Hurd, the British Minister of State and Robert Wade-Gery, the British High Commissioner-designate to Delhi. I had a brief talk with Douglas Hurd, whom I had known earlier, about the activities of some of the leaders of the insurgency movements in the North-Eastern States who were then living in the U.K.

The Prime Minister and party stayed at the Carlyle Hotel at New York. I had a meeting in my suite with the advance team which had been in Washington to finalise the brief for the Prime Minister on the issues for discussion with the President and his team.

On the 28th the Prime Minister visited the U.N. and presented a fifteenth century sculpture of the Sun God, Surya to the United Nations. Mr Perez De Cuellar, the new Secretary-General of the U.N., received the gift at a brief ceremony which was attended by an enthusiastic gathering of over 300 special invitees.

The Prime Minister and party reached Washington at 5.40 p.m. on the 28th and were received by Secretary of State Schulz at the Andrew Air Force base and from there we were taken to Washington by helicopter. According to the protocol practice in U.S.A., the Secretary of State receives the visiting VIP first and later the VIP is given a ceremonial welcome by the President when he arrives at the White House lawns.

The ceremonial reception at the White House on the 29th morning was a very colourful one. We reached the White House lawns at 9.30 a.m. and stood at our allotted places. Sonia and children were at the head of the front line followed by G. Parthasarathi and me and Ambassador K.R. Narayanan. Rajiv took his position a couple of feet in front of us. The special invitees stood in several rows behind us to the right of the platform. The TV and press corps were on the left side and the troops who were to present the guard of honour and the band had been smartly drawn up in front of the platform. It was an exceptionally bright day and the ceremonial uniforms of the soldiers and the band group and the bright colours of the Indian Women's sarees lent great charm and variety to the ceremony at the lush green lawns of the White House. At 9.58 a.m. the President and Nancy Reagan arrived in front of the White House walking from within the house and took their position at the edge of the road. In a minute, the limousine carrying Indira Gandhi moved in and she was received by a hearty handshake by the President and escorted to the platform. Nancy Reagan took Rajiv by hand and they stood together a few feet in front of us.

There was great warmth and cordiality in the words of the President's welcome address and his behaviour. President Reagan is well known for his showmanship on such occasions and it is difficult not to be impressed by his performance. Indira Gandhi in her red silk saree presented a picture of dignity and grace. The speeches by the two heads of government were followed by a very impressive march by the soldiers dressed in eighteenth century-style uniforms. The President and the Prime Minister then moved into the White House for a tete-a-tete and the rest of the party assembled in another room for discussions.

The greatest irritant in the Indo-US relations at that time was the sudden decision of the U.S. Government to discontinue supplies of enriched uranium to the atomic power plant at Tarapore. According to a legislation passed by the U.S. Congress, the U.S. authorities sought to impose some new conditions on India in return for the facility of continued supply of enriched uranium. The supplies for Tarapore were getting exhausted and India was facing the difficult option of either having to shut down Tarapore or to accept the new conditions. The U.S. side realised the moral strength of the Indian stand that the U.S. should not impose fresh conditions or modifications in an on-going agreement based on a new decision of the Congress. However, the administration persisted in its efforts to pressurise us on this issue hoping that India would agree to give the necessary assurances to meet the U.S. Congress's new guidelines.

Dr. Sethna, Chairman, Atomic Energy Commission, Krishnaswamy Rao Saheb, Cabinet Secretary, M.K. Rasgotra, Foreign Secretary and I had been engaged in negotiations on this subject with the U.S. side for some weeks prior to the Prime Minister's visit. We had several talks in Delhi with the U.S. Ambassador Harry Barnes and on all such occasions we had made it clear that we would not accept any condition or obligation beyond what had been stipulated in the 1963 agreement during the pendency of that agreement which was till 1993. Finally we had arrived at an arrangement by which supplies would continue uninterrupted while the U.S. government could also technically take the stand that it was not violating the resolution of the Congress. We had taken the compromise formula reached at Delhi as final and did not except any further controversies on this subject. However, the day after our arrival in Washington a news item quoting well-informed sources in the State Department appeared in the U.S. press that India had given up the right of reprocessing the spent fuel in return for the continued supply of the fuel from a third source. This statement put us in an embarrassing position and Rasgotra and I immediately sought a meeting with Mr Murphy, Under-Secretary of State in the State Department, to seek clarifications. We explained to Murphy that India continued to retain the right to reprocess the spent fuel and that under no circumstances would we agree to accept any conditions of the type reported in the U.S. press. The laboriously constituted Delhi agreement appeared to be in serious danger. However, after long discussions, both sides agreed that we could proceed on the basis of the formula reached at Delhi. We were happy that we did not have to accept any new interpretations or obligations in return for continued supplies. In later meetings with the U.S. officials and with President Reagan, the Tarapore issue was not raised at all except to record satisfaction that a satisfactory solution had been found for this problem.

While the President and the Prime Minister were having their one-to-one talk without any aides, Mr Schulz, Secretary of State, met our delegation in an adjoining room. He asked us to explain the basic principles and policies governing our development programmes. What he was specifically interested in knowing was the role assigned to the public sector in our development programmes. I briefly explained the main policies and priorities of India's development programmes and the role of the government in ensuring that the scarce resources of the country are deployed to meet priority requirements through the mechanism of planning. While we were in the midst of the discussions on this subject, we were called in to join the President and the Prime Minister for the plenary session.

The President was assisted by Vice-President Bush, Secretary of State Schulz, Treasury Secretary Regan and a few other senior officials. After some preliminary remarks from the President and the Prime Minister, talks centered mostly on economic issues. The subjects which came up prominently were the future of IDA, India's right to borrow from the Asian Development Bank, and the importance of concessional aid as against commercial credit for India's development needs. The Prime Minister asked me to explain our stand on each of these issues and the President and his colleagues sought some further clarifications on my comments and observations. Except for some comments of a general nature by the President, most of the searching questions were put by Schulz. The discussions were held in a very cordial atmosphere, though the U.S. side did not show any inclination to make any change in their known stand on these issues. The U.S. attitude had been particularly unhelpful to India and even self-contradictory in certain matters. On the IDA loans, the U.S. wanted the claims of new applicants such as China to be accepted, while on ADB loans their stand was that since India had not availed of these loans earlier, the claims of the old borrowers should be protected first. There was then the familiar homily about the virtues of borrowing from commercial banks, leaving the development agencies to cater to the needs of the more needy countries. Even before the talks started, we knew that the U.S. government would not make any concessions to India on these issues. The results were as we expected. We had gone to the meeting with little expectation and therefore we had no serious disappointment. On the other hand, we had the satisfaction that we could point out to the highest policy-making levels in the U.S. some of the obvious contradictions in their stand on lending by IDA and ADB. The plenary session lasted about an hour and a half and we left for a lunch hosted there by Mr Schulz in honour of Indira Gandhi at the State Department.

I should mention here a small incident about Donald Regan, Treasury Secretary, which caused some avoidable misunderstanding. Regan wanted to have a separate meeting with the Prime Minister. Some of us who knew his clout in the administration, particularly in decisions on financial matters, had strongly recommended to the Prime Minister that she should receive him in a separate meeting. But for some inexplicable reasons she did not agree. She felt that it was adequate that she met him along with others on other occasions like the plenary meeting at the White House or the lunch with Schulz. Regan I did not quite like this and never forgot this unintended slight, as was clear from the unhelpful attitude of the Treasury Department in all matters affecting India in subsequent months.

On the 29th afternoon, the Prime Minister addressed the Foreign Affairs Committee of the Senate and the Congress. There were many friends and sympathisers at this meeting, but there were also some critics who still considered India as a Soviet client. The questions and comments from these quarters were not very friendly.

The high point of the visit was the banquet hosted by the President at the White House on 29th night. The President and Mrs Reagan received the guests at the East Room and then we went to the State Dining Room. It was a glittering show with all the top Washington elite present. The speech by the President exhibited extraordinary warmth for India and it looked as if Reagan had decided to start a new policy of friendliness for India. The banquet was followed by an orchestra conducted by Zubin Mehta at the lawns of the White House. We left the White House at 11 p.m. while other American guests continued with their dance and music.

On the 30th, Indira Gandhi visited the *Washington Post* for an off-the-record interview. As directed by her, I explained to the senior editors the issues involved in the Tarapore dispute and the main points of the agreement arrived at with the U.S.

The National Press Club lunch for the Prime Minister was a memorable event for many reasons. The hall was packed to capacity and we were told that the organisers had to turn down several requests for seats for the paid lunch. Some of us had a rather unpleasant experience while we were on our way to the venue of the lunch. Rajiv, Sonia, Natwar Singh and a few others in the Prime Minister's party, including me, were caught in a lift which got stuck between the first and second floors. Suddenly, the lights in the lift went off and it stopped moving. One of the security guards with us had a walkie-talkie with him and, therefore, he could communicate to the people outside about our rather unenviable position. After fifteen minutes, the lift was manually brought down to a position from where we could jump out. The lift was a bit overcrowded and I saw Natwar Singh perspiring profusely in a state of claustrophobic nervousness. When the lift was lowered, he was the first to jump out, Natwar told me later that he would have collapsed if help was delayed by a few more moments.

On 30 April, we attended a reception at Ambassador K.R. Narayanan's residence, where the Prime Minister met a large number of Indians in Washington. The Prime Minister hosted a dinner for Vice-President Bush and other U.S. leaders.

On 31st forenoon we attended a meeting organised by the Indian community at the Kennedy Center which was packed to capacity. We returned to New York by noon. The Prime Minister met a group of Indian businessmen and another of Indian scientists at the Carlyle Hotel, where we were staying. In both the meetings I was asked to explain India's policies for attracting investment and technical collaboration.

There was an interesting incident when Indira Gandhi and three or four of us went to see the play *Agnes* at a New York theatre. I was sitting immediately behind Mrs Gandhi and a man sitting next to me suddenly fainted and collapsed to the floor. Within seconds, the U.S. Secret Service Personnel sprang out from nowhere and formed a ring around the Prime Minister's seat while others quietly removed the man. There was no foul play involved, but I was quite impressed by the alertness of the U.S. Secret Service in coping with that situation.

I noticed the same alertness and sense of duty on their part on another occasion during this visit. All members of the Prime Minister's delegation had been given identification badges, which we were expected to wear always. One morning, I was suddenly called by the Prime Minister to her room and in the hurry to get there, I forgot to wear the badge. The Secret Service man on duty near her room politely told me that he knew I was an important member of the Prime Minister's party, but would still ask me to go back to my room to wear my badge before he could let me into her room. I was full of admiration for his sense of duty and promptly complied with his demand.

On 1 August, the Prime Minister and her party visited the Gurudwara in New York. A batch of Sikh demonstrators carrying placards took their stand at about fifty yards from the Gurudwara and kept shouting slogans against her and the Indian government. The meeting inside the Gurudwara was intended to welcome Indira Gandhi, but even on this occasion, the main speaker could not resist the temptation of referring to the so-called injustice and disabilities experienced by the Sikh community in India. The Prime Minister spoke with great dignity and restraint and said that they should learn to think of India before their community or state.

The highlight of the engagements on 2 August was a lunch hosted jointly by the Asia Society and the Foreign Policy Association at Waldorf Astoria. There were 1,600 guests for the lunch and we were told that over 800 applicants had to be denied admission because the hall was already overcrowded. Indira Gandhi's ready wit and humour in answering the questions made a favourable impact on the audience and there was loud applause from the floor at every reply. The loudest applause was when she replied to the question "Which way do you tilt – towards the West or the East?" She snapped in reply: "We stand upright".

On 2 August, we left for Los Angeles. We saw a small group of Afghan demonstrators shouting slogans against India in front of the Century Plaza Hotel at Los Angeles where we were staying. There was a civic reception for the Prime Minister the next day and we left for Honolulu soon after.

At Honolulu, the Prime Minister presented a baby elephant, which had been flown out from India earlier to the zoo at a very colourful ceremony in the park. We left for Tokyo on the 4th afternoon after a hectic programme of over one week.

The brief stay in Tokyo on 4 and 5 August was not an official visit, but was in the nature of a stop-over. There was a pleasant meeting with Prime Minister Suzuki of Japan, followed by a dinner hosted by him in honour of Mrs Gandhi. Suzuki was very warm in his reference to the Prime Minister while proposing the toast. He said that Indira Gandhi was not only a great leader of Asia and the developing world, but the leader of the whole world.

Back in India, on 6 August, after an absence of nearly a fortnight, everyone expected the Prime Minister to make a statement on her visit in the Parliament which was then in session. But in spite of advice from some of us, she refused to make a statement personally and instead asked P.V. Narasimha Rao, the Foreign Minister, to do so. Narasimha Rao was not even in her entourage during the visit and the Opposition did not take to this arrangement kindly. There were loud protests and shouts in Parliament culminating in a walk-out by the Opposition. This decision is again somewhat inexplicable. Some of us felt that she should have personally made a statement as she had come back after a very important visit but she maintained that it would establish a wrong precedent and therefore, refused to accept our advice on this.

The Soviet Union : 20-26 September 1982

Ever since the signing of the Indo-Soviet Treaty of Friendship and Co-operation in 1971, India's non-alignment had become somewhat suspect in the eyes of the western world. Indira Gandhi had been asked by several visiting western leaders and journalists as to why India had chosen to enter into such an agreement with the USSR, particularly on defence matters. Indira Gandhi's consistent reply had been that co-operation in economic and defence matters did not in any way compromise India's policy on non-alignment and India would continue to keep its independence in foreign relations.

I have heard her on several occasions explaining to visitors from the west as to how the U.S.A. rejected the proposal made by India in the 50s for bilateral assistance in starting a steel plant in the public sector. The U.S. was the first country approached by India for assistance for starting a steel plant but it refused on the ground that it could not co-operate with a public sector project. India, therefore, turned to the Soviet Union for collaboration in starting a steel plant and it readily extended its co-operation. Again, the arrangements for trade with the Soviet Union based on the bilateral balancing principle had the built-in advantage of promoting Indian exports. India paid for the goods imported from the Soviet Union by its exports to that country and this did not cause any drain on its foreign exchange resources. In the matter of defence equipment also India had received special treatment from the Soviet Union. It was quite willing to extend technical co-operation in the manufacture of defence items in India unlike some western countries which were reluctant to transfer their technology. In spite of the favourable treatment India received from the Soviets, the bulk of India's trade and economic co-operation had been with the west.

A common criticism against Indira Gandhi's non-aligned policy was that India's votes on various resolutions in the United Nations had been cast on most occasions against the U.S. stand and in favour of that the Soviet Union. Indira Gandhi's reply to this criticism was that India never voted for or against the U.S. or the Soviet Union. It exercised its vote consistent with its own policies and interests. If the stand taken by the U.S. on various issues happened to be against the stand of India and most other non-aligned countries, as was often the case on subjects like the Palestinian cause, apartheid, the New International Economic Order, etc., India could not be blamed for it. Indira Gandhi objected to the condescending attitude of the big powers looking at the exercise of votes by the weaker countries as votes either for or against them. These were votes for or against a particular proposition based on its merits, irrespective of the support or opposition by the big countries and that, she maintained, was the essence of non-alignment.

The Soviets never raised any criticism against India even though India had often differed with their stand on various issues. They had shown greater understanding of India's policy of non-alignment than the west had.

The Soviets always wished to treat India as if it enjoyed a special status of friendship among the countries outside the COMECON. Senior ministers from the Soviet Union visiting India missed no opportunity to stress the special bonds of friendship between India and their country and the need for further strengthening such co-operation. India had been particularly grateful to the Soviet Union for its consistent support to its stand in its disputes with Pakistan. The Soviet Union had shown great understanding of India's policies and even when it differed with our stand on certain issues, it respected our position and did not allow such differences to affect the friendly ' relations between the two countries. Personally, Indira Gandhi was held in high esteem by the Soviet leaders and a visit by her to their country was naturally treated as an event of very special importance. It was in this background of great friendship and warmth of relationship that the Prime Minister's visit was taking place in September 1982.

There were no special irritants in the Indo-Soviet relationship, nor any special problems which had to be sorted out at the heads of government level. There were some issues like terms of credit, etc., on which the officials of the two countries had been having discussions, but they were expected to be sorted out at the sessions of the Joint Commission or at other such levels. Indira Gandhi's visit to the Soviet Union was intended purely to re-emphasise the prevailing friendship and understanding between the two countries and to assure each other of the importance attached by both sides to such continuing relationship.

The Indian delegation to the USSR included Rajiv Gandhi, P.V. Narasimha Rao, G. Parthasarathi, myself and a few officers from the ministry of External Affairs and the Prime Minister's Office. We arrived at Moscow at 12.30 p.m. on 20th September and were received at the airport by a large team of Soviet leaders headed by President Brezhnev. Brezhnev had been ailing for some months and everyone knew that his physical and mental faculties were not as sound as they used to be. Brezhnev walked smartly along with Indira Gandhi as she inspected the guard of honour at the airport, but we could easily detect an awkwardness in his gait and visible faltering in his steps. We were driven to the Kremlin Palace where Mrs Gandhi and the senior members of her delegation were being accommodated. Seeing the luxurious suites which had been allotted to us in the Kremlin Palace, I wondered whether we were in a Marxist country at all. Mrs Gandhi and Rajiv had their suites in one wing of the Kremlin while the rest of us were in another wing. Indira Gandhi's suite had a very large and luxurious sitting room next to the bedroom, where she could receive visitors or hold meetings.

The first meeting of the two delegations was held in the afternoon of 20 September. Brezhnev read out a long speech and the Prime Minister also made a speech from a written text. In reading the speech and later in the discussions at the plenary session, Brezhnev gave the impression of a robot acting entirely on buttons pushed from elsewhere. He displayed no emotion on his face; in fact, his face appeared totally lifeless. He would often ask Prime Minister Tikhanov or Foreign Minister Gromyko in loud tones as to what was being said then and it was very clear to those of us watching him that he was not able to follow the discussions clearly. Gromyko was often seen whispering – it was really shouting – into his ears what was being said but he did not show any indication of following what was being discussed. It was indeed a pathetic sight to see this once powerful leader of the Soviet Union in this state of a corpse-like existence. There must have been very valid and important reasons for keeping up this charade, even though everyone near the centre of power in the Soviet Union should have known that the centre was no longer capable of functioning.

The State banquet at the Kremlin on the 20th night in honour of Indira Gandhi was a magnificent show of splendour and lavishness. The banquet hall with its gilded walls, priceless paintings and huge chandeliers presented the appearance of a fairy land. Brezhnev-watching again became my preoccupation at the banquet. He did not take any of the alcoholic drinks which were served in front of him at the table; in fact he hardly ate or drank at the banquet. He read his speech, again like a robot, and did not show any sign of his being part of the activities which were going on in the hall.

The second plenary session on 21 September was, in contrast, a most businesslike one. The Soviet team was led by Tikhanov, who was quite knowledgeable on all aspects of Indo-Soviet relations.

On the 22nd, the Soviet Foreign Minister, Gromyko had a meeting with Indira Gandhi in the sitting room adjacent to her suite at the Kremlin and the two had a very extensive review of world developments. Gromyko had an interpreter to assist him, but he followed English clearly and when he occasionally spoke in English, he did so effortlessly. P.V. Narasimha Rao, G. Parthasarathi and I were present at this meeting to assist Mrs Gandhi. It was quite an experience to be present when two of the world's most knowledgeable persons on international affairs were having a very relaxed and intimate exchange of views.

After the conclusion of the talks in Moscow, Mrs Gandhi and her party visited Tallinin in the Baltic region and Kiev, one of the largest industrial cities of the Soviet Union. In both places, large crowds lined up the streets waving Indian flags and we could see great warmth and enthusiasm in their welcome.

The visit to the Soviet Union served its purpose adequately – the strengthening of Indo-Soviet friendship. We returned to Delhi on 26th evening.

Brezhnev, whom we found so ill when we took leave of him, was to survive only for a few more months.

1983

Belgrade, Helsinki, Copenhagen, Oslo, Vienna
8-19 June 1983

Belgrade, Yugoslavia

After a break of nearly nine months, I was again accompanying Indira Gandhi on her foreign visits, this time to five countries in Europe. The first place of visit was Belgrade, capital of Yugoslavia, a country with which India had very close relationship in the days of Nehru and Tito. Mrs Gandhi had visited Belgrade a few times earlier and these visits had always been very pleasant experiences for her. But Yugoslavia after Tito was an entirely different country. Tito could give this loose association of different nationalities with widely differing levels of development a sense of unity and a well-knit identity by the sheer strength of his charisma and leadership. His heroic exploits in fighting the Nazis during the Partisan days and the courage he had shown in defying the authority of the all-powerful Stalin in the post-independence years had made him a superhero in the eyes of his people and he dominated the political scene of Yugoslavia unquestioned during his lifetime. But the new Constitution of Yugoslavia which made the Presidency rotate for short periods among the members of the Presidium had considerably weakened the authority of the President within and outside the country. The serious economic problems which it had to face led to the further erosion of its international importance and influence. Still Yugoslavia, as one of the founder-leaders of the Non-Aligned Movement, had a special place of regard and respect in India, and Indira Gandhi's visit was intended to strengthen this decades-old special friendship. The immediate purpose of her visit was to attend the United Nations Conference on Trade and Development (UNCTAD) which was being held at Belgrade and to deliver the Raul Prebisch lecture, for which she had been invited.

The Prime Minister was accompanied by Sonia Gandhi, Rahul and Priyanka. The Prebisch lecture was delivered to a fully packed hall at the UNCTAD session on the evening of 8 June and was acclaimed by delegates from developing countries as a bold and masterly presentation of the case of the Third World before a world audience. It was a hard-hitting speech, critical of the lack of understanding shown by the developed countries about the needs and interests of the poorer nations. It was somewhat sharp in its comments on the rigidities in the working of the international financial institutions. Later in the evening, there was a State banquet at the Palace of Federations and at the reception preceding the banquet, De la Rossier, Executive Director of the I.M.F.,Dunkel, Director-General of the GATT and Clausen, President of the World Bank told me that they were unhappy at the tone and thrust of Mrs Gandhi's speech. They said that they were surprised at her remarks about the international financial institutions and thought they were rather harsh. Perhaps, they expected that India, which was the largest beneficiary of financial assistance from these institutions, would be more generous in her assessment of their role. I explained to them that Indira Gandhi had in no way exaggerated the gravity of the situation in most developing countries or the sentiments of disappointments and frustration in these countries at the stalemate in the North-South dialogues. However, I felt that they should get the reply to their comments directly from her and I took them to the corner of the reception room where she was standing. Indira Gandhi told them that when she spoke about the problems and frustrations of the developing countries, she was not speaking on behalf of India alone but as the spokesperson of the majority of these countries. At the meetings of the Non-Aligned Movement, she had some times to present the views of the northern countries on North-South issues to ensure a balanced understanding of their policies, but at international conferences like the UNCTAD, she had to articulate the deeply-felt views of the South. She said that there was no point in overlooking the seriousness of the crisis faced by the poor nations, but her comments were to be taken as a basis for a meaningful dialogue and not as condemnation of any institution or group. Her listeners did not appear to be quite convinced, at any rate, not Mr. De la Rossier, as he continued to talk on the Prime Minister's comments at the table where I was sitting along with him, Dunkel and Clausen for the dinner. However, most of the delegates were very happy at the forthright manner in which she had put forward the case of the developing countries.

On 9 June, Indira Gandhi addressed the Yugoslav Parliament, which was again a special occasion to emphasise the close ties of friendship between the two countries and to recall the great services of Nehru and Tito to the Non-Aligned Movement. We left Belgrade for Helsinki on 10 June.

Helsinki, Finland

In many respects Finland is an unusual place, different from numerous other countries I had visited along with Mrs Gandhi. In its economic and foreign policies, Finland had been trying to follow an independent course. Finland had to live with its special relationship with the Soviet Union and there was some lack of credibility about its independence in foreign policy. Though a Scandinavian country, it was different from its other Nordic neighbours as it had to maintain a delicate balance between the realities of its special links with the Soviet Union and its aspirations to be completely independent of foreign influence.

The names of places and persons completely baffles a new arrival in Helsinki. The hotel we stayed at was called KALASTAJATORPPA, the wreath-laying ceremony was at HIETANEIMI cemetery and the splendid music concert we attended, at the TEMPPELIAKIO church. I realised that it would be a totally unrewarding effort for any Indian visitor to try to pronounce the Finnish names even remotely correctly.

One of the items included in the Prime Minister's schedule was a cruise in the Baltic on board an ice-breaker. We thought it was intended only as a pleasure trip, but soon discovered that the Finns were very keen to sell such a vessel to India as we were at that time looking for an ice-breaker for the Antartica Expedition. There was a lot of sales talk by the Finns accompanying us on this cruise to some of the members of the Prime Minister's party, and we could not help feeling that this was a plain mixing of business with hospitality.

Copenhagen, Denmark

The visits to the Nordic countries were mainly in the nature of goodwill visits. There were no bilateral problems for discussion. The Scandinavian countries had been generous in their aid to India and had been quite appreciative of the efforts made by India in preserving democratic institutions in contrast to what was happening in our neighbourhood.

We landed at Copenhagen to a tumultuous welcome by the small but extremely enthusiastic Indian community in Denmark. There was also a small group of Pakistanis from occupied Kashmir at the airport with their placards of protest.

The first impression I got on arrival at Copenhagen was the extreme informality of those in authority in the country. Prime Minister Schuller and his wife were quite informal and relaxed in their attitude to Indira Gandhi and I noticed this mood of friendliness in the welcome by the ordinary people as well. There was a dinner in honour of Mrs Gandhi at the famous amusement park at Tivoli Gardens and during the magnificent fireworks which were a part of the entertainment, a huge welcome sign appeared in the sky with the words SU SWAGATAM INDIRA in Devanagri letters.

Among the places visited in Copenhagen was the home of Hans Christian Andersen which is now a museum attracting large number of visitors. On the 13th we had official talks with the Danish Prime Minister and his ministers and lunch with Queen Margarette II of Denmark at her Palace.

Oslo, Norway

On arrival at the Oslo airport, we saw a small group of Ananda Margis carrying placards and shouting slogans against Indira Gandhi and her government. We were never made to forget the conflicts and cleavages back in Indian society even on our visits to very remote countries.

The informality of Scandinavian welcome and hospitality was equally evident in Oslo. On the 15th Mrs Gandhi had talks with the Norwegian Prime Minister at the Parliament House. This was followed by a press conference.

We were guests of King Olav V at his Palace for lunch. As we reached the front gate of the palace, we saw the King arriving there himself driving the car. He was completing 80 years in a few days, but was in such good health that he appeared 20 years younger. We spent the 15th night at Lofthtis, which we reached travelling by plane and helicopter. At the old castle-like hotel where we were staying, we were entertained to some lively Norwegian folk dances. A wonderful and unforgettable experience of the visit was a tour of the famous Hardenger Fjord on a Norwegian frigate. The beauty of the Baltic Sea surrounded by snow-capped mountains was indeed breathtaking.

We left for Vienna on the 16th afternoon.

Vienna, Austria

There was a large gathering of Indians at the airport to welcome Mrs Gandhi on arrival at the Vienna airport on the 16th evening. One of her important engagements in Austria was a talk at the India-EEC Dialogue at Alpbach, which was a largely attended conference of European and Indian businessmen. But an equally important mission for her was to meet the former Austrian Chancellor Kreisky, who had been a personal friend of Nehru and Indira Gandhi for several years.

We reached Innsbruck by plane – it was only an hour's flight from Vienna – on the 18th and from there proceeded by car to Alpbach. Innsbruck is a well-known Austrian tourist resort and large crowds of tourists had thronged to this place hearing about Indira Gandhi's arrival there. She was mobbed by enthusiastic crowds as she moved around the place along with Mr Kreisky and the Austrian security men had quite a job clearing the road for her. Kreisky travelled with her from Innsbruck to Alpbach and back and this gave her adequate time to talk to him about matters of common interest.

In her address at the India-EEC Dialogue Mrs Gandhi explained India's policies regarding foreign investment and technological co-operation. We returned to Vienna on the 18th evening and boarded the Air-India plane for Delhi. We were back in Delhi on the 19th morning after an absence of eleven days.

Cyprus, Greece, Paris, New York
20 September – 4 October 1983

Cyprus

Cyprus, a small island of less than a million people had always had a prominent place of honour in the group of non-aligned nations, quite out of proportion to its size or economic potential. This was largely the contribution of that charismatic personality, Archbishop Makarios, who had endeared himself to Nehru, Nasser and Tito and other founding fathers of the Non-Aligned Movement by his indomitable courage and firm commitment to non-alignment. President Kyprianu was a good friend of Mrs Gandhi and therefore, a visit to Cyprus was of special personal interest to her.

When we arrived at the Larnaca airport at 12 noon on the 20th, it looked as if the entire population of the island had turned up to welcome Indira Gandhi. The route from the airport to the Hilton hotel where we stayed was lined by Cypriot citizens and school children waving Indian flags and loudly shouting "Gandhi, Gandhi". On the 21st morning, Indira Gandhi was the guest of a civic reception at the Town Hall. This was followed by a ceremony for naming a prominent avenue near the Parliament House as Jawaharlal Nehru Avenue. The Cypriots had a few years earlier installed a bust of Mahatma Gandhi at this place. By naming this avenue after Jawaharlal Nehru, the association of this place with India got further strengthened.

We left for Athens on the 22nd.

Athens

On the evening of the 22nd we had official level talks with the Greek ministers and senior officials and later the two Prime Ministers joined the talks. Prime Minister Papanadreau was the current President of the EEC and the talks, therefore, covered Indo-EEC relations, besides bilateral issues. On the 23rd, President Karamalis hosted a lunch in honour of Indira Gandhi at the Presidential Palace. In the evening, Indira Gandhi visited the Acropolis with some of us.

On the 24th we went by helicopter to Delphi and visited the famous site of the Delphi temple and of the Oracle. On return to Athens we saw a Greek play, *Oedipus Rex,* in a traditional Greek Open Air Theatre. We left Athens for Paris on the 25th. During our visits to the Acropolis, Delphi and the Open Air Theatre, we were escorted by Greece's charming Tourism minister and well-known actress Melina Mercouri. Indira Gandhi thoroughly enjoyed her company and later told us that she was quite impressed by the versatility of her interests and knowledge.

Paris

The halt at Paris was for less than a day. President Mitterrand hosted a dinner for Mrs Gandhi on 25th night and she availed of this opportunity to ask his advice about the main issues for focus at the mini-summit of a group of heads of government which she had convened at New York. President Mitterrand was of the view that the focus should mainly be on economic issues such as reform of the monetary system, development aid, etc., rather than on political issues. In fact, this was what Mrs Gandhi also had in view while taking the initiative to convene this conference. The talks between President Mitterrand and Mrs Gandhi were entirely in French and an interpreter sitting by my side was helping me follow the talks and also translating my remarks and comments into French. Among the six persons at the dinner I was the only one who could not speak French.

New York

The main purpose of the Prime Minister's visit to New York was to address the UN General Assembly. Since a large number of heads of government were visiting New York at that time for the same purpose, she had in her capacity as chairperson of the NAM, convened a meeting of some of them for a mini-summit to review the progress in the on-going North-South dialogue.

Immediately upon arrival at New York, we had lunch with the senior editors of the *New York Times*. During the lunch they asked a number of questions on the recent liberalisation introduced in our economic policies and I was asked to give them the explanations and replies. Mrs Gandhi was very frank and forthcoming in explaining our stand on various issues as the whole talk was intended to serve only as background information.

On the afternoon of the 26th, Mrs Gandhi called on President Reagan at his suite in Waldorf Astoria. The President and the Prime Minister met alone for a short time and we were later called in for general discussions. As on the two previous occasions, when I was present with the Prime Minister for her meeting with President Reagan, I found Reagan a very disinterested participant. Most of the talking was done as usual by Secretary of State Schulz. The only time I noticed the President to be lively was when he sharply condemned the action of the Soviets in shooting down a Korean plane.

On the 26th evening, Mrs Gandhi addressed a meeting of heads of the delegations of Non-Aligned countries at the U.N. The meetings of the heads of government convened by the Prime Minister were held in two sessions at the UN, the first on the 27th and the second on the 29th. About twenty heads of government attended these sessions and very actively participated in the discussions. The most active participants were President Mitterrand of France and President Julius Nyerere of Tanzania.

On the 28th Mrs Gandhi addressed the UN General Assembly. Her address attracted more than the usual attention of the delegates and the media because of her position as the Chairperson of NAM. She spoke not only on behalf of India but as the spokesperson of the Non-Aligned Movement on all matters of concern to the developing countries.

Mrs Gandhi's other engagements in New York included an address at the Indian Overseas League and an interview on NBC TV. We left for London on the evening of 2nd October and after a brief halt in London, reached Delhi on 4th October.

This was the last occasion I was to accompany Indira Gandhi on a foreign visit. During 1984, her foreign visits were few and even those she undertook were brief. One was a visit to Moscow for a day in February to attend the funeral of President Andropov and the other, a two-day visit to Libya and Tunis in April 1984.

4

INDIRA GANDHI AND MGR

Indira Gandhi's relationship with the non-Congress - I Chief Ministers was always cordial. She had known Jyothi Basu and Ramakrishna Hegde long before they had become Chief Ministers in West Bengal and Karnataka respectively and had no problem in continuing friendly relationship with them. N T Rama Rao was relatively a stranger to her and a newcomer to politics when he became Chief Minister of Andhra Pradesh, but she could establish an easy rapport with him. Farooq Abdullah was always treated by her with great affection and regard as a member of her family though there were patches of strain for a very brief period in their relationship. Indira Gandhi's relationship with M G Ramachandran or MGR as he was popularly known, the charismatic Chief Minister of Tamil Nadu, had however a different history. It was quite strained at the time of her return to power in 1980, but after a few meetings and frank discussions between them it developed into one of great trust and respect for each other. As one who was associated with these discussions I should relate here the facts about the manner in which misunderstandings were cleared and close friendship developed between them.

During the Janata rule Indira Gandhi had thought of contesting a by-election to the Lok Sabha from the Thanjavur constituency in Tamil Nadu and MGR had offered his party's support for it. But he later withdrew the offer reportedly under pressure from Prime Minister Morarji Desai. Indira Gandhi decided not to contest this by-election, but MGR's action had rankled in her mind. Some important ministers in MGR's cabinet and senior functionaries in his party had been making vicious attacks on Indira Gandhi in their speeches and writings and these continued unabated even after her return to power. There were a few interested persons in the Tamil Nadu Congress Party also who did not like MGR coming close to Indira Gandhi. They made it a regular practice to furnish to her English translations of some of the rabid anti-Indira and anti-Congress speeches and articles by some of MGR's close confidants and to tell her that these speeches were being made on the instructions of MGR himself.

Once, while she was travelling to Madras in September 1981, an MP from Tamil Nadu who was travelling with her in the same plane, gave her the translations of a few very foul anti-Indira speeches by one of MGR's ministers. Indira Gandhi was quite annoyed that such personal attacks could be made by a minister against the Prime Minister. I was accompanying her on this visit and she sent for me in her cabin and showed me those papers with undisguised anger.

MGR had come to the airport to receive her, but her attitude was very cold on meeting him. MGR's car was part of the cavalcade to the Raj Bhavan, but well behind the car in which the Prime Minister was travelling. The Prime Minister suddenly asked her car to stop before it had left the airport gates and asked me to request MGR to travel with her in her car. MGR was somewhat taken by surprise at this sudden request but readily joined her.

To put it mildly the talk that followed was not pleasant. Indira Gandhi expressed her great annoyance at the nasty attacks on her by MGR's ministerial colleagues and asked him plainly why he was encouraging such personal attacks against the Prime Minister. MGR did not want to carry on an argument on this subject in the car. Further, he had difficulty in expressing himself in English that too at a time when he found Indira Gandhi in a really agitated mood.

Later, upon reaching the Raj Bhavan, MGR told me that he resented very much the tone and manner of Indira Gandhi's talk to him. He said he felt very embarrassed at this sudden expression of annoyance by the Prime Minister and that he kept quiet in the car only because he did not want to create any unpleasantness. As regards the offending speeches and articles, he said that neither he personally nor his party subscribed to such views and if any minister had indulged in such foul language, he would certainly pull him up and see that there would be no further repetition of such speeches. He added that he was aware of the machinations of some people from Tamil Nadu to create a rift between him and Indira Gandhi and that I should inform her about such designs. He said that he had always held Indira Gandhi in high esteem and it was his desire to maintain cordial relations with her if she too also wished likewise.

MGR was genuinely keen to be a good friend of Indira Gandhi's, and to establish direct contacts with her, but he also wanted to eliminate the intermediary role of certain Congress-I leaders from Tamil Nadu, some of whom he greatly disliked. I promptly conveyed these views to Indira Gandhi and told her that if she chose to deal directly with MGR, there would be no cause for any misunderstanding. Much to my surprise, I found that she retained no bitterness after that unpleasant talk in the car. It was only a sudden expression of annoyance, but one without malice. She told me that she had no doubt at all about MGR's personal regard for her and that she wanted to reciprocate it with equal warmth and cordiality.

I conveyed Indira Gandhi's feelings to MGR and he felt happy that the misunderstanding had been cleared. However, no further initiative was taken during this visit to improve her relations with MGR.

Indira Gandhi encouraged me to play an active role in removing the misunderstanding between her and MGR and in bringing them closer. In the subsequent months they had a number of meetings. In the first few meetings MGR used to be accompanied by S. Ramachandran, his Minister of Electricity. Later MGR used to come alone to meet Indira Gandhi and I was the only other person present at these meetings, acting as an interpreter for Indira Gandhi's English into Tamil and MGR's Tamil into English. Obviously, MGR wanted these talks to be kept strictly at a personal level and did not want even a trusted colleague like Ramachandran to be present.

With every meeting their regard for each other grew and they soon became good friends, with great respect for each other. The question of an electoral alliance was never discussed at these meetings. It was not Indira Gandhi's style to hold direct talks with anyone on matters like electoral alliances, seat adjustments, etc. She believed that her role was to establish friendship and understanding at the higher levels and that the follow-up action on electoral alliances etc., should be done by others at the appropriate stage. MGR had no difficulty in getting the message that she was in favour of an electoral alliance between her party and the AIADMK when the occasion arose. MGR himself continued his meetings with her on the understanding, though not specifically spelt out, that both sides welcomed such an alliance.

I recall an interesting conversation between Indira Gandhi and MGR which showed the warm and relaxed level their relationship grew into. While discussing a delicate political matter at the Raj Bhavan, Madras, during her visit there in April 1983, Indira Gandhi who was in a very happy mood, said: "I really do not know what to do about this. CM, you are a very shrewd and mature politician and you should suggest a good solution". When I translated this to MGR, he promptly replied in Tamil: "Amma says I am a shrewd and mature politician. Who am I before her in political shrewdness? Where is an ant-hill and where is Mount Everest?" When I conveyed these words in English to Indira Gandhi, she laughed heartily at the eloquence and ready wit of MGR. However, after claiming that he was only an ant-hill before Mount Everest in political shrewdness, MGR went on to suggest various options available for a solution to the problem posed by Indira Gandhi and recommended a particular option as the best in his judgement. She told him that she agreed with his suggestion fully and thanked him profusely for his advice.

The friendship between the two steadily improved and Indira Gandhi grew to develop great respect for the political maturity and leadership qualities of MGR. She used to discuss with him not only matters relating to Tamil Nadu or the problems of Tamils in Sri Lanka, but other important national issues like the agitation by the Akalis and by the students in Assam. She was greatly impressed by MGR's understanding of the mind and mood of the common people on various sensitive issues and the candidness with which he offered advice on them. She looked upon MGR as a great champion of national unity and integrity and felt confident that she could rely on his support in any situation of national crisis. MGR in turn was all admiration for her cosmopolitan and truly national outlook, particularly for the manner in which she defended the rights of the non-Hindi language groups against the excessive zeal of certain Hindi enthusiasts.

The news of MGR's sudden illness was a great shock to Indira Gandhi. She was at her office on 16 October 1984, when the message reached that MGR had suffered a stroke and that his condition was causing anxiety. She immediately initiated enquiries about getting the services of specialists from the U.S.A. or U.K.

and told us that she would like to fly to Madras to see MGR as soon as arrangements could be made.

G. Parthasarathi and I accompanied Indira Gandhi on that flight, leaving Delhi at 1.30 p.m. As instructed by the Prime Minister, I had telephoned Governor Khurana that he and the ministers should not bring flowers or garlands to the airport and also requested him to inform those coming to the airport not to raise slogans in support of her as was the usual practice. From the airport she drove straight to the Apollo Hospital and saw MGR lying seriously ill in his bed. Huge crowds had gathered at the hospital and had also lined up along either side of the road when news spread that Indira Gandhi was visiting MGR. G. Parthasarathi and I went inside the room along with Mrs Gandhi. When she went near the bed MGR recognised her and wanted to sit up to welcome her. He motioned to his doctors to raise him, but Mrs Gandhi asked him to keep on lying and not exert himself in trying to get up. She then told him: "CM, please look after yourself well and get well quick. You have fought many battles in your life and have shown great courage all your life. You will show the same courage in this crisis too". MGR appeared deeply moved and tried to say something, but could not speak. Mrs Gandhi talked to Mrs Janaki Ramachandran for a few minutes and after a meeting with the doctors left for Raj Bhavan to meet the ministers of the Tamil Nadu government. We returned to Delhi the same evening. This turned out to be the last of the several meetings MGR had with Indira Gandhi.

5

THE PRIME MINISTER AND THE PRESIDENT

Indira Gandhi and President Sanjiva Reddy

When Indira Gandhi returned to power in January 1980, she had a new Parliament, a new cabinet and new Legislative Assemblies and councils of ministers in most states, but she had to work with the incumbent President, Neelam Sanjiva Reddy, who had been elected as the Janata Party's nominee and whose earlier attempt to enter Rashtrapati Bhavan had been effectively thwarted by none else but herself. Sanjiva Reddy himself had become disillusioned with the infighting among the top leaders of the Janata government. However, while he felt relieved that the country had at last an effective administration with the return of Indira Gandhi to power, neither he nor Indira Gandhi could easily forget the bitter politics of the previous decade when the two were powerful adversaries. There was, therefore, a conspicuous absence of a relaxed relationship between the President and the Prime Minister. They were quite correct in their dealings with each other, but the undertone of strain and coldness was there for any one to notice.

Sanjiva Reddy had strongly disliked the dominant influence of Sanjay Gandhi in the early months of the Indira administration and had little rapport with most of her new cabinet ministers and chief ministers who had come to wield political influence and power in the post-Janata period. While he had no regrets about the fall of the Janata government, he had no enthusiasm either for the new brand of political leadership that had emerged and kept lamenting to any willing to listen about the sad decline of standards from the Nehruvian heights. Indira Gandhi was quite aware of the fact that the President had become openly critical about her style of administration and more so of her ministerial colleagues, but took them as inevitable problems of adjustment and was willing to live with this situation for the remaining period of Sanjiva Reddy's presidency. She was determined not to precipitate any crisis or provoke any confrontation. The President was also keen to maintain the best of relationship with the Prime Minister in spite of the obvious strains and tensions beneath the surface.

I had the privilege of knowing Sanjiva Reddy when he was a minister at the Centre. Before leaving Delhi in June 1978 to take up my assignment with the UN in Geneva, I had made a farewell call on him at Rashtrapati Bhavan and I had received great kindness and courtesy from him on that occasion. I found that he had been well informed about the circumstances in which I had to leave my post as Secretary in the Ministry of Commerce. He spoke to me with great sympathy and consideration about the treatment which had been meted out to me. I was greatly touched by his kindness and affection.

Within a few days of my taking over as Principal Secretary, I called on the President to pay my respects. He then told me that he was quite pleased that I had come back to the government in a more important position and this showed that integrity would always get its recognition. He told me that it was my duty to express my views to the Prime Minister frankly and fearlessly in all situations, which would be the best way of serving her. He said that all sorts of people were trying to play the role of adviser to the Prime Minister but most of them had their own axes to grind and he was confident that with me in the position of Principal Secretary, the Prime Minister would get honest advice on all matters. From the way he repeatedly mentioned the need for giving frank and honest advice on all matters to the Prime Minister, I could guess that he had some reservations about the role of some of the Prime Ministers close colleagues. Very soon I was to know more about the tensions in the relationship between the two high dignitaries of the country.

By about the end of 1981, President Sanjiva Reddy had become very critical about the working of the government and had been expressing his views rather frankly to people who called on him. His five year tenure was to come to an end by the mid-July 1982 and he knew very well that Indira Gandhi would not favour a second term for him. In fairness to him, it should be said that he never expressed any interest in a second term or tried to ascertain the Prime Minister's likely reaction to such a proposal. He knew exactly where he stood in his relationship with the Prime Minister and had made it known that he was not a candidate for a second term. A few people took special delight in carrying to the Prime Minister highly coloured versions of what the President reportedly said about some particular government decision or about the general style of its functioning. Sanjiva Reddy was not always very restrained in his comments and observations and, therefore, there were enough opportunities for rumour-mongers to do their mischief.

By about January 1982, there were strong rumours in Delhi that the President had become quite unhappy at the manner in which the administration was being carried on and that he felt that the Prime Minister had been deliberately slighting him and also that he had every intention of asserting his constitutional rights and duties. The mischief makers went to the extent of informing the Prime Minister that the President would soon provoke an open confrontation with her and ask for her resignation and, in case she refused, would even dismiss her. I had also received such reports, but had not taken them seriously.

A few days before the Republic Day, Indira Gandhi asked me whether I was aware of such reports and whether I had initiated necessary action to meet all eventualities. I could see that Indira Gandhi was not taking those rumours lightly. Having gone through very bitter experiences in life, including her own expulsion from Parliament and her imprisonment, nothing was unthinkable or improbable in her calculations and, she was therefore, not inclined to dismiss these reports as inconsequential. Krishnaswamy Rao Sahib, Cabinet Secretary, R.N. Kao, Chief of the Research and Analysis Wing, T.N. Chaturvedi, Home Secretary and I held several meetings to consider the implications of these reports. Though we were all convinced that these rumours were largely the creation of interested individuals, we did not wish to dismiss them as entirely improbable and, therefore, started checking on each report and rumour with great thoroughness and care.

It was in this background that everyone eagerly waited for the Republic Day address which the President was to broadcast on the night of 25th January 1982. There were strong rumours that the President's address would be highly critical of the administration and that it would be a public indictment of the Prime Minister before the people, forcing an open break in their relationship.

It was customary for the President's secretariat to prepare the draft of the President's Republic Day address and send it to the

Prime Minister's office for clearance by the Prime Minister. She had asked me to obtain the draft well in advance so that there would be adequate time to go through it and suggest revisions, if found necessary. I had requested V.K. Rao, a retired ICS officer of the Andhra Pradesh cadre, whom the President had appointed as his Principal Secretary, to send me the draft at least two clear days before the 25th and Rao had said that he would try to do so.

I received the draft of the President's speech at 7.15 p.m. on the 23rd of January at my office in the South Block and on going through it my worst fears were confirmed. The draft was highly critical, if not condemnatory, of the working of the government during the last one year and I knew that the Prime Minister was not going to accept this. I was quite upset at the thought of an imminent confrontation between the President and the Prime Minister and after sidelining the paragraphs which in my judgement were sharply critical of the government, I rushed to Indira Gandhi's office to show her the draft.

As soon as I entered her room with the text of the speech in my hand, she guessed that things had gone wrong. She kept looking at me and could see that I was visibly disturbed. I told her that I was quite unhappy at the tone of the draft and that some paragraphs would definitely require revision. I then passed on the text to her and requested her to go through it and particularly see the portions I had sidelined. She did not read the text, but only glanced through the portions sidelined by me and that too very quickly. She then returned it to me and said, "I do not have to read it. I knew from your face as soon as you entered what it contained". She then said in a very emphatic tone: "This speech is not going to be broadcast in this form". I requested her again to read the text but she merely said: "You have read it carefully and you have told me what it contains. There is no need for me to read it now. What is important is to consider quickly the next step to take". I was greatly worried at her defiant stand and suggested that a meeting of the Cabinet Committee on Political Affairs (CCPA) might be called immediately to consider the draft and to suggest amendments. She instead asked me to take the draft to R. Venkataraman and P.V. Narasimha Rao immediately for getting their views and then to see her later at her residence.

I called on Narasimha Rao first and later Venkataraman and showed them the draft. After carefully reading the text, both, expressed the view that the speech was damaging to the government and that it would initiate quite an embarrassing practice were the Head of the State to condemn his own government and that, too, through a Republic Day address to the nation. They said that the speech had to undergo substantial revision and that a meeting of the CCPA should be convened immediately to consider this matter. When I reached the Prime Minister's house, Pranab Mukherjee was already there. I reported to the Prime Minister the views of Venkataraman and Narasimha Rao about the draft and she said that a new draft should immediately be prepared. The CCPA was to meet the next morning to consider the revised draft. After getting CCPA's clearance of the revised draft, she would meet the President and request him to adopt the text as approved by the CCPA. She did not say what she would do if the President refused, but it was very clear to me that she was fully prepared to take a strong stand on this issue.

Sharada Prasad and I discussed the lines on which the draft could be revised. We felt that the format and content should be as close to the original as possible, but that all condemnatory references to the government should be replaced by non-offending formulations. Sharada Prasad, an expert in the art of drafting and editing, did an excellent job and produced a draft early on the morning of the 24th of January, retaining the main points of the original draft more or less intact, but without its offending tone and language. The CCPA met in the morning and cleared the draft.

The Prime Minister then sought an immediate appointment with the President and 1 p.m. was indicated as the time convenient to the President. Asked by Indira Gandhi, I accompanied her in her car to Rashtrapati Bhavan. She went into the President's room with the revised draft while I waited with great anxiety and concern in the adjacent room. At 1.40 p.m. they both came out of the room and from the smile on Indira Gandhi's face, I could guess that a crisis had been averted. I accompanied her in her car to her residence and in the car she told me that everything was under control. After reaching her house, she told me that the President thought that there was nothing condemnatory of the government in the original draft, but had agreed to the revised draft brought by her. When the speech was broadcast on the 25th night many thought that it was very critical of the government, but few knew the efforts and anxiety that had gone into the revision of the original draft.

Sanjiva Reddy was very particular that all courtesies due to his high office should be extended by the Prime Minister without even the slightest lapse. On her part, Indira Gandhi was meticulous in these matters and seldom departed from the strict code of protocol so far as the courtesies due to the President were concerned. However, there were a few occasions when the President thought that there were lapses on her side, though these instances would have passed off unnoticed had the relationship between them been more relaxed and cordial. One such occasion was when the Prime Minister could not be present at the airport to receive the President who was returning from a State visit to Ireland on the 10th of May 1982. His plane was to land at 9.45 p.m. and Indira Gandhi had returned to Delhi after a hectic election tour only an hour or so earlier. She was not feeling well that evening, and therefore, decided to take rest. She wrote a letter in her own hand apologising for her inability to be present at the airport and asked me to give the letter personally to the President with appropriate explanations on his arrival. I did that, but the President was visibly unhappy at her absence.

A week earlier, there had been another minor incident. The King of Nepal was on an official visit to Delhi and the President wanted to host a dinner in his honour. Indira Gandhi herself was hosting a lunch in honour of the King on the same day and she wanted to excuse herself from attending the President's dinner. The President's secretariat was informed that the Prime Minister would not be coming for the dinner. The President's Secretary asked me whether I could make a special request to Indira Gandhi to attend. The Prime Minister had, in the meanwhile, fixed up some other important engagements and was reluctant to change her schedule. The President was obviously unhappy at the Prime Minister declining his invitation for the dinner. Her absence at the airport to receive him, though it was because she was unwell, aggravated his unhappiness.

How sensitive Sanjiva Reddy was on matters affecting the status and authority of the President can be seen from another controversy which arose in connection with a visit to Jammu and Kashmir which he had planned to make. The visit was scheduled for the first week of June 1982, but the J&K Resettlement Bill, on which Chief Minister Sheikh Abdullah was very keen, had roused a good deal of controversy and strong public criticism and some ministers of the central government thought that it would not be advisable for the President to visit the state at that time. This matter was being discussed among themselves by some ministers and Justice Madhusudhan Rao, Chairman of the Monopolies and Restrictive Trade Practices Commission, who was known to the President and who came to know of this matter, took upon himself the responsibility to advise the President to postpone his visit. The judge apparently thought highly of his friendship with the President and felt that this was a matter on which he might render advice. He committed the further mistake of dropping Shiv Shankar's name to the President which created the impression that he was conveying this message on behalf of Shiv Shankar also. Justice Rao obviously acted in good faith, but Sanjiva Reddy was furious at this unsolicited advice and particularly at Rao trying to speak also on behalf of Shiv Shankar in a matter with which neither was concerned. The President's Principal Secretary informed me that the President was quite displeased at this unwarranted interference by others and their unsolicited advice and that I should report this to the Prime Minister, which I did. Shiv Shankar told me later that he had not asked Madhusudhan Rao to speak to the President and Rao had acted entirely on his own.

The new President, Zail Singh, was to be formally sworn in on the 25th of July 1982 and friends and supporters of President Sanjiva Reddy were expecting as a matter of normal course that the Prime Minister would take the initiative of honouring him with Bharat Ratna. A fortnight before the President was to lay down his office, Rao, his Principal Secretary, asked me and the Cabinet Secretary whether any move was being made in this matter. I knew quite well that Indira Gandhi had no such intention. Nevertheless, I brought this to her notice and she, as expected, did not take any initiative.

In spite of the undercurrent of strain in the relationship between the Prime Minister and the President, the farewell functions were marked by great warmth and cordiality. On the 25th of July at the solemn function at Rashtrapati Bhavan when Sanjiva Reddy moved from his chair and invited Zail Singh to take that seat, he appeared quite relaxed, even relieved. He was equally dignified and relaxed at the formal departure ceremony later in the day at the airport.

Indira Gandhi and President Zail Singh

The meteoric rise of Zail Singh to the highest office in the country was in many respects an unusual phenomenon in the political history of independent India. This was not, as many seem to think, because of the fact that he was a person with very little formal education or qualification. In fact, such qualifications are not essential for high political offices in a democracy. Others without the benefit of formal education have also risen to high positions in public life in India, and few considered it strange. Kamaraj and Vasant Rao Patil became Chief Ministers of two premier states of the country and proved to be two of the ablest chief ministers of independent India. Kamaraj, who spoke neither Hindi nor English, became the President of the Indian National Congress at a time when the Congress party had very eminent intellectuals of great political standing, highly eligible for occupying such a position. But Kamaraj and Vasant Rao Patil, though not educated in the formal sense, were men of great charisma who grew to be the obvious choices for the eminent positions they came to occupy. Very few at that time felt that there was anything unusual in their holding these positions. However, when Zail Singh was selected as the Congress party candidate for the post of President, many could not accept that choice as either natural or obvious. The party took it without any demur, or even the semblance of a debate, because the choice was made by Indira Gandhi whose opinions alone then counted in such matters in the party. The choice came as totally unexpected, but it was also fully accepted because of the pre-eminent position in the party of the person who made the choice.

It would be unfair to Zail Singh to say that he manoeuvred for this position. In fact no aspirant could have done any maneuvering for himself even if he wanted to. At a later stage when it became clear that Indira Gandhi was seriously considering Zail Singh's candidature, some of his supporters helped reinforce his candidature by making some adroit moves, which I shall discuss later in this chapter. After several days of serious thinking, Indira Gandhi clinched the choice in Zail Singh's favour as he appeared to her to be the right choice for the post in the circumstances which prevailed in the country in 1982 and Indira Gandhi's choice became the party's choice.

I have said earlier that Indira Gandhi herself had at one time thought of retiring from active politics and offering herself as a candidate for Presidentship. For about a fortnight during May 1982, she seriously considered the pros and cons of this proposition but she gave up all such thoughts by the end of May and started examining the suitability of others for this post.

One day early in June 1982, in the midst of my discussions with Indira Gandhi on some official matters, she suddenly asked me as to what the general view was about the proper candidate for the post of President. I was not surprised by such a question as I knew her style very well by then. It might sound strange to others that the Prime Minister should discuss such an important political issue with a civil servant functioning in her office, but as I have said earlier, it was always her practice to pose such issues for my reactions, and I was used to such questions. On such occasions, I used to express my views freely and frankly as I knew that was what she expected from me.

I had known earlier that Indira Gandhi had no intention of fielding Vice-President Hidayatulla as the candidate for the Presidentship. If he was to continue as the Vice-President, I presumed that, according to the conventions in selections to the offices of President and Vice-President, the next President should be from the South. I could not think of any one from the South more suitable than P.V. Narasimha Rao and R. Venkataraman and I straightaway said that these two would be seen by the public as right choices. R. Venkataraman had just taken over as Defence Minister after having been Finance Minister for over two years and I knew from my earlier talks with Indira Gandhi that she would not think of another change for him at that stage. I, therefore, said that the candidature of P.V. Narasimha Rao would be seen as the most acceptable by the people. I knew that she would never take a risk on the issue of loyalty and Narasimha Rao was ideally suitable on this criterion. His long experience as minister and later Chief Minister at the state level, the senior positions he had held in the Congress party at various stages and the success he had made of his stewardship of the ministry of External Affairs made him stand out as one of the most eligible among the ministers to hold this prestigious position. His intellectual attainments and vast scholarship were other plus points. But his main drawback was his political rootlessness. Though elected from Andhra Pradesh, he had not taken the trouble of maintaining close contact with his home state and had, in fact slowly drifted away from Andhra politics. Therefore, there were no influential groups to speak up for him.

Indira Gandhi's first reaction was that he was very useful to her as a minister and should serve for some more years as a minister before being considered for a position which meant virtual retirement from politics. Still, she said that he would be an ideal candidate on grounds of merit and general acceptability. At that stage, she seemed to be thinking of making a selection from the South and Narasimha Rao appeared to her the most eligible candidate for the post.

On some subsequent occasions, Indira Gandhi mentioned the name of Narasimha Rao as the person she was seriously considering as the Party's candidate for Presidentship and I got the impression that she had made up her mind in his favour.

But, by about the middle of June, I noticed a shift in the Prime Minister's thinking about Narasimha Rao. Once while discussing the choice for the Presidential election, she mentioned the name of Zail Singh as another person whom she considered quite suitable for the post. I then realised that what I had thought till then to be a mere gossip in the corridors of South Block had really engaged the active consideration of the Prime Minister. She especially mentioned his shrewdness and sagacity as a politician and said that the convention regarding representation to the South could be taken care of when the vacancy for Vice-Presidentship arose later.

It came indeed as a surprise to me that Zail Singh's name was being so seriously considered by her. My personal relationship with Zail Singh had been very good. As Home Minister, he had always shown me great courtesy and I was grateful to him for his kindness and affection. But I knew Mrs Gandhi was drawing me out and using me as a sounding board. These were occasions when I had to express my views frankly, as otherwise, I would not be doing my duty to the Prime Minister. I, therefore, plainly told her that if she were to propose Zail Singh for the Presidentship, it would be seen as purely motivated by political considerations and that she would come in for a lot of criticism on this score.

In subsequent discussions I got the impression that she had not finally made up her mind and was still in the process of weighing the pros and cons of the idea. In fact, on one occasion she even told me that she was seriously considering possible candidates as

Minister for External Affairs if Narasimha Rao were to be elevated as President.

But events were moving very fast in favour of Zail Singh. Perhaps one of the important considerations which weighed with Mrs Gandhi in his favour was her calculation that his elevation as President would please the Sikh community. No Sikh had so far held the post of President or Vice-President and she probably thought that the Sikh community would consider Zail Singh's elevation as a gesture of goodwill to it. In spite of all her shrewdness as a politician and her intimate grasp of the nuances of Punjab politics, she was very soon proved wrong in thinking that the Sikh community would feel particularly gratified at Zail Singh's selection as President. On the other hand, his choice was seen by most Sikhs as motivated by Indira Gandhi's wish to have a pliable person in Rashtrapati Bhavan.

An important development which finally helped clinch the matter in favour of Zail Singh was the declaration of support by some chief ministers and prominent political leaders of the South for his candidature, in preference to Narasimha Rao. Some of these senior leaders from the South met Indira Gandhi separately and told her that Narasimha Rao's selection would not be seen by most people in the South as the selection of a true South Indian. The specious argument advanced by them was that, since Rao was a Brahmin, he would not be a proper representative of the people of the South where anti-Brahmin sentiments were very strong. Some of them even told her that, as between Narasimha Rao, a Brahmin and Zail Singh, a Sikh from a backward non-Brahmin caste, the people of the South would prefer the latter. None of these leaders had consulted their colleagues in their party on this before giving such advice to the Prime Minister. They were actually conveying to the Prime Minister their own views, though they made them appear as the views of the majority of the people of the South. When Indira Gandhi mentioned this to me, I knew how this so-called spontaneous expression of support for Zail Singh from the South had come about and who had been behind this move. I did not say anything about it to her, as I realised that by then she had made up her mind in favour of Zail Singh and the expression of support by the leaders from the South only served to strengthen her belief that she had after all made the right choice.

P.V. Narasimha Rao himself was not a candidate for the post. In fact, he had taken the philosophical attitude that, if Indira Gandhi wanted him to be President, there was little that he need to do in the matter. On the other hand, if she did not want him to be the President, there was little that he could do either. Narasimha Rao was most of the time away on his travels in foreign countries during these crucial days and did not even know of the moves that had been made against him by some chief ministers and party leaders from the South.

Once Indira Gandhi had made known her personal preference in favour of Zail Singh, his endorsement as the candidate of the Congress party was a mere formality. With the overwhelming majority which the Congress party then commanded in the electoral college. Zail Singh's election as President was a foregone conclusion, and on 25 July 1982 Zail Singh became the new occupant of Rashtrapati Bhavan.

Indira Gandhi had fondly hoped that, with Zail Singh's elevation to Presidentship, some of the problems which had cropped up in the Punjab administration would automatically get resolved. She had been very unhappy at the undercurrent of hostility which marked the relationship between Chief Minister Darbara Singh and Zail Singh as Home Minister and which had started affecting the smooth running of the day-to-day administration of the state. Zail Singh had been very bitter about what he thought were the deliberate efforts on the part of Darbara Singh to reverse and even discredit some of the programmes he had introduced during his Chief Ministership of Punjab. Darbara Singh, on the other hand, maintained that Zail Singh had not been able to forget his old Chief Ministerial role and had been trying to interfere in the Punjab administration. Even after Zail Singh's assumption of office as President, Darbara Singh kept on complaining to Mrs Gandhi about what he called attempts at remote control from Delhi.

The conflict between the two became unfortunately most evident in the matter of handling the Akali agitation and later the terrorist activities by the Punjab administration. The President felt that the Chief Minister was not dealing with the situation tactfully and that the Chief Minister's policies were only leading to further alienation of neutral Sikh opinion from the government. His criticisms of the Chief Minister became increasingly sharp and strident as the law and order situation in Punjab started deteriorating.

Darbara Singh continued to enjoy the full support of the Prime Minister in spite of Zail Singh's strong disapproval of his handling the situation and Zail Singh felt very unhappy about this. This made him more annoyed with Darbara Singh. What was worse, he started expressing his annoyance at the policies and action of the Prime Minister herself rather openly. To some senior ministers and party leaders he expressed his displeasure at his not being consulted by the Prime Minister on various measures taken by the government to deal with the Punjab agitation.

Indira Gandhi kept the President informed of all steps taken to handle the agitation and also about the secret talks that were being held between the Akali leaders and the government. However, she received reports that some people in the President's office were maintaining close contacts with certain groups of extremists in Punjab and she felt quite unhappy about it. These persons did not have any unpatriotic motives, but they probably thought that it was prudent for them to maintain contacts with the agitators to keep the lines of communication open. However, this caused a great deal of annoyance to the Prime Minister as she felt that those working in the President's office should not get involved in such matters. From then on, she became somewhat cautious and restrained in conveying to the President details regarding the secret negotiations with the Akali leaders and her own strategy for dealing with agitators in Punjab, and this caused a good deal of unpleasantness.

In the meanwhile, the Punjab situation was fast deteriorating and terrorists were literally getting away with murder. There were loud protests from all over the country about the failure of the Punjab government to prevent these shocking acts of violence, and more so, about its failure to apprehend the culprits.

The proverbial last straw was the horrible incident of the hijacking of a Punjab roadways bus by the terrorists and the killing of six Hindu passengers on 5 October 1983. Darbara Singh was summoned to Delhi on the 6th evening and told by the Prime Minister that in the prevalent situation in the state, there was no choice but to impose President's rule. He was quite unhappy at this suggestion and pleaded for more time to set matters right. A.P. Sharma, the Governor, who arrived in Delhi along with Darbara Singh, was quite happy and relieved to know that he was to be replaced by B.D. Pande, who was then Governor of West Bengal.

As directed by the Prime Minister, I met the President at 8.15 p.m. on 6 October and apprised him of the changes which she was considering in Punjab. Later that night the Cabinet met and decided to recommend to the President that Punjab be brought under President's rule and the President signed the proclamation the very same night. Needless to say, the President was quite pleased at this decision.

The general expectation that the Punjab situation would be brought under control by the imposition of President's rule was soon proved wrong. Violence continued to escalate and the senior leaders of the Akali Dal got practically sidelined by the extremists. The control of the Golden Temple, though nominally under the Shiromani Gurdwara Prabandhak Committee (SGPC) had, *de facto*, passed on to the hands of the extremists. Public opinion in the country had become very critical of what was seen as hesitation on the part of the government to use adequate force against the militants and there was persistent demand for military action. Throughout this period, negotiations were being held by the government with the leaders of the Akali Dal in an effort to find a peaceful settlement, but it became clear that even if a settlement could be reached with the Akali leaders, it might not be binding on the militant groups. The Prime Minister had been regularly briefing the President about the progress of the negotiations and the senior ministers participating in them also kept the President informed about the details of the talks. The President continued to express his unhappiness at the manner in which the agitation was being handled, though he himself did not offer any specific suggestion as to what else or more should be done.

Indira Gandhi was greatly concerned about the continued criticism from the President and used to tell some of us that she had expected from him greater understanding. There was a marked escalation in the tone of the President's criticism of the Prime Minister's policies after the army action in Amritsar. Indira Gandhi in turn felt very unhappy that, of all persons Zail Singh, whom she expected to be a pillar of support at a time when she was being subjected to a great deal of criticism by several Sikh leaders, should have himself assumed the role of a sharp critic. She knew that Zail Singh was quite shaken by the military action and that the reports of the damage to the Akal Takht and the killing of innocent people in the temple had particularly disturbed him. Indira Gandhi showed great understanding about the emotional upset which Zail Singh was going through as a religious person at that time and therefore refrained from talking to him about her own sense of hurt, though she talked about this often with great feeling to some of us.

When the President visited the Golden Temple on 8 June 1984, he turned his anger on Governor B.D. Pande who was accompanying him on this visit. He rebuked the Governor of gross negligence in his duty. Pande was quite shaken by this undeserved rebuke, but being an experienced and disciplined civilian, he kept his cool.

Zail Singh was scheduled to preside over the National Films Award ceremony at Vigyan Bhavan, Delhi, but he was so upset by his visit to Amritsar that he decided not to attend this function. Indira Gandhi was informed about this decision and some of the organisers suggested that she should persuade the President to keep the engagement, as its cancellation might lead to unpleasant speculation in the press. But she did not wish to request the President to change his decision as she wanted to respect his feelings in this matter. There were rumours in Delhi that the President had written to the Prime Minister tendering his resignation, but in fact, no such letter was sent by him.

After the army action, Zail Singh came in for very severe criticism from the Sikh community. They accused him most unfairly of personal responsibility for ordering the military operation as he was the supreme commander of the armed forces. Ordinary people are not quite informed about the decision-making processes in the central government in such a situation and they cannot be blamed if they believed that orders for the army action were issued by the President personally in his capacity as the supreme commander. This type of undeserved criticism by fellow Sikhs aggravated his uneasiness.

Now a more serious development personally affecting Zail Singh took place, which further disturbed him. While negotiations were going on between the Sikh priests and the government representatives about the terms and conditions for the handing over the control of the Golden Temple to the priests, on 2nd September 1984 the priests took the drastic step of declaring President Zail Singh and minister Buta Singh as *Tankhaiya*, or outside the Sikh faith. The Akalis fixed 30 September as the deadline for withdrawal of the army from the Golden Temple and announced that there would be statewide agitations from that day if their demand was not accepted.

The Prime Minister knew that Zail Singh was quite upset by the excommunication order and did not want to do or say anything which would hurt his feelings. However, Zail Singh was not just a member of the Sikh community, he was the President of the country and she was anxious that the prestige and importance of his high office should not in any way be compromised. She wished that the whole issue be handled at a political plane and wanted to initiate negotiations with the priests for a package agreement covering all matters including transfer of the Temple to the control of the SGPC. But it soon became clear to her that Zail Singh did not want anyone else to interfere in the excommunication issue which he wanted to deal with himself, delinking it from other issues connected with the transfer of the Temple.

P.V. Narasimha Rao, Home Minister, called on the President immediately after the *Tankhaiya* action was announced by the priests. In his talk with Rao, the President, was unusually severe in his criticism of the government's action. He told him that the government had bungled in the handling of the agitation and was particularly vehement in his condemnation of the role of Darbara Singh in the past and of Governor B.D. Pande and his advisers. And then he came out with a strong indictment of Indira Gandhi, which was totally unexpected. Narasimha Rao was taken aback by the severity of the criticism about the Prime Minister. The President knew very well that his remarks would be conveyed to the Prime Minister. Perhaps this was what he wanted, and Rao did so promptly.

The Prime Minister felt very hurt when she received the report of Rao's meeting with Zail Singh. However, she thought that Zail Singh must have been in an emotionally disturbed state and did not wish to talk to him immediately to refute his allegations. She called on the President on evening of 4 September and reassured him that the government was doing everything possible to restore normalcy in Punjab. The President did not display any unpleasantness during his meeting with the Prime Minister. The meeting was an unusually brief one, but from then on Indira Gandhi was convinced that a great change had taken place in the attitude of the President towards her and felt quite unhappy about this.

The Indian Express carried a report on 5 September from its special correspondent, who was well-known in Delhi as a person close to the President's office, containing a fairly correct account of Zail Singh's talk with Narasimha Rao. We were quite concerned that a conversation between the President and the Home Minister could be made known to the public through the columns of the press. The President's secretary telephoned me to say that the President was unhappy at the press report and that he was writing to the Home Minister contradicting the report. But the harm had been done and the public, which till then had only heard vague rumours of a rift between the President and the Prime Minister, now started believing that a rift did exist in fact.

In the meanwhile, efforts were being made to reach a settlement with the Akalis about the handing over of the management of the Temple to the priests. The renovation of the damaged Akal Takht was proceeding at top speed and it was the government's intention to withdraw the army from the Temple as soon as the repairs were completed. But Indira Gandhi was very particular that there should be an undertaking on the part of the priests that they would not allow the Temple again to be used by the militants for their activities. The government also expected that, as part of the overall settlement, the priests would withdraw the *"Tankhaiya"* action against Zail Singh, Buta Singh and Baba Santa Singh who was leading the "Karseva" for repairs to the Akal Takht.

While these talks were going on, the President decided to visit the Golden Temple. The Prime Minister was definitely for postponing the Presidents visit till the priests accepted the condition of forbidding the use of the premises of the Temple by the extremists and till the Temple itself was finally handed over to the SGPC on the basis of that undertaking. However, the President was in contact with the priests and had decided to visit the Temple without waiting for the government to conclude the agreement which it was trying to negotiate. This completely upset the strategy which Indira Gandhi had about the transfer of the Temple to the priests after getting an undertaking from them; however, she did not want to try persuading the President to postpone his visit again. Instead, she decided to announce the transfer the control of the Temple to the SGPC before the President visited the Temple and the news was broadcast on the night of 25 September. The priests announced the lifting of the *"Tankhaiya"* action on Zail Singh on

26 September, but did not revoke the action against Buta Singh or give any undertaking about preventing the misuse of the Temple. The undertaking was obtained later, but only after several rounds of painstaking negotiations and even then in a somewhat diluted fashion.

Zail Singh visited the Golden Temple on 27 September but the occasion was used by the priests to show their hostility to the government and gross disrespect to the President. None of the priests received him on arrival at the Temple gate; instead he was received only by government officials and some Congressmen and was escorted to the Temple where the priests had assembled. He had an hour's meeting with the priests privately. The priests then accompanied him to the Akal Takht and to Harmandir Sahib. After offering his prayers, he addressed the congregation in the Temple and then he was to face a very embarrassing situation. Kripal Singh, the Chief Priest, did not want to miss the opportunity of the presence of the President of India in the Temple for mounting a severe attack on the government and the Indian army. Kripal Singh spoke after the President had spoken, and therefore the President was not prepared for the condemnation. He listened in silence, though with evident unhappiness, to a severe indictment of the government and the conduct of the army. He asked the Governor at the airport while leaving Amritsar to convey his displeasure to the priests.

There was strong criticism in the press about the conduct of the priests and also about the fact that the President himself did not speak out to refute the allegations against the army. The mood of resentment in the country was eloquently brought out by veteran journalist Nikhil Chakravarthy in an article entitled *In a China Shop* where he said: "All the perfumes of Arabia cannot wash out the stink caused by the President's failure to say at least one sentence in defence of the Jawans". In defence of Zail Singh, it has been said that he refrained from speaking again after Kripal Singh's speech as he thought that it would only lead to an unseemly debate inside the Temple.

Indira Gandhi felt outraged when she received the report of what had transpired at the Temple, but she said nothing about this to the President. She knew that he felt very unhappy at the incident, but the decision to visit the Temple before an agreement could be reached with the priests was entirely his and she did not want to aggravate his bruised feelings. However, the warmth and trust which characterised their relationship during the early part of the Presidency had by now vanished and instead there were visible signs of strain.

Zail Singh left on a state visit to Mauritius on 22 October 1984 and by this time his relationship with the Prime Minister had touched a level of coolness and distrust. Indira Gandhi was at the airport to see him off. I was talking to her at the airport when the President's car arrived. She received him and walked along with him to the lounge where other VIPs were waiting to meet him. After walking with the President a few paces from the place where he alighted from the car, she suddenly stopped about midway to the lounge. I then saw Indira Gandhi and Zail Singh engaged in a very serious talk for about three to four minutes. I was just a few feet away from them and could see very clearly from Mrs Gandhi's face that the talk was not a very pleasant one. After seeing the President off, Mrs Gandhi herself left on a visit to Uttar Pradesh from the technical area of the airport. I had no opportunity to talk to her again at the airport.

After her visit to U.P., Indira Gandhi suddenly decided to visit Kashmir and I met her on her return from Kashmir on the evening of 28 October at her residence. She then spoke to me with some anguish about what she described as the growing coldness in Zail Singh's attitude towards her, in spite of her doing her best to accommodate his personal sentiments to the maximum extent possible. She said that she could not understand what exactly he wanted. She then asked me whether I had noticed her talking to Zail Singh at the airport while he was leaving for Mauritius. I said I had and thought that the talk was not a very pleasant one.

She then narrated to me exactly how the talk went between them. She said that she told Zail Singh that she was quite unhappy at his changed attitude towards her. Zail Singh replied that he had also reasons for unhappiness, but would like to talk to her about this matter when they both had the time. She told him that they had talked enough and wondered whether there was anything more to talk about. Zail Singh was surprised at this remark and at the tone of her talk and that too on the occasion of his departure to a foreign country. He then told her, "If I come back alive after this visit, I would have a lot to speak to you on this subject". Indira Gandhi was taken aback by the words "If I come back alive" and she quickly concluded the talk telling him that he was in perfect health and should not be talking in these terms when he was proceeding on a foreign journey.

I was indeed puzzled that she chose to talk to Zail Singh in such plain terms about her unhappiness at the change in his attitude at a time when he was taking leave of her to go on a foreign visit. As she always expected me to give my reactions frankly, I told her that I felt she should have chosen another occasion for such a talk. She replied in a very serious tone "I felt that I had to talk to him plainly, and therefore, I did so". She again said grimly : "I had to do it and I did it".

When Zail Singh mentioned to Indira Gandhi at the airport on 22 October that he would talk to her at length about the strains which had developed in their relationship if he came back alive from his foreign tour, little could he have expected that he would not be seeing her alive again.

6

THE LAST DAYS

Concern at Pakistan's support to secessionists

While the problem of secessionism in Punjab continued to be Indira Gandhi's main preoccupation for in the last few months before her death, she was equally worried by the sudden spurt of anti-national and secessionist activities in Jammu and Kashmir. The support which the secessionists had been getting from Pakistan in the form of training and supply of arms and the manner in which anti-national elements could easily secure safe sanctuaries in Pakistan caused her great concern. In spite of reliable evidence the government had in its possession of Pakistan's assistance to the Sikh extremists, she did not want to make any public accusation against Pakistan at that stage, as she believed that this matter should be taken up with the Pakistani authorities through diplomatic channels. The White Paper on Punjab published by the government went to the extent of saying that the government had reason to believe that the terrorists were receiving active support from certain foreign sources. It said: "The significant relationship between internal and external forces of subversion is a well-known fact of the contemporary international scene. However, it would not be in the public interest to divulge information which the government has on this aspect of terrorism in Punjab." This statement showed how cautious the government was at that stage in openly charging Pakistan with complicity in the secessionist activities in Punjab. The White Paper had also referred to the nexus between Sikh extremist organisations based in foreign countries and the organisations supporting secessionism in Jammu and Kashmir. It had mentioned the fact of close contacts between Chouhan of the Khalistan National Council and the leaders of the J&K Liberation Front and between the members of Dal Khalsa and the leaders of the "Azad" J&K Muslim Conference. Pakistan's support for these organisations in their common objective of promoting secession was well-known to the government and was becoming a major source of strain in Indo-Pakistan relations.

On 25 October 1984, Humayun Khan, Pakistan's Ambassador in Delhi, came to see me to discus this subject. Normally, he should have seen the Foreign Secretary or the Minister of External Affairs for such discussions, but he told me that he had been asked by President Zia to convey his concern over the deteriorating relations between the two countries directly to the Prime Minister through me and said that the main purpose of his meeting with me was to inquire whether the Prime Minister would be agreeable to resumption of talks with the President.

I knew clearly the Prime Minister's mind on this subject, and therefore told the Ambassador that what India was looking for was some tangible evidence of a change in Pakistan's attitude towards India and that resumption of talks would become meaningful only in such circumstances. I told the Ambassador about the damage that was being caused by Pakistan's support to terrorist activities in India and the vicious anti-India propaganda that was being carried on in the official Pakistani media. I mentioned the fact that the extremists who had hijacked Indian planes were still enjoying Pakistan's hospitality and this was causing great resentment in India. I also told him that we had evidence of the hijackers getting a pistol from the Pakistanis after they had landed in Pakistan and how these incidents were aggravating the strains in our relations. The Ambassador denied the charge of the supply of a pistol to the hijackers. I pointed out to the Ambassador that it was not our intention to allow these complaints to become the subject of public controversy, but Pakistan should at least return the hijackers to our authorities as a token of their keenness to restore good relations with India. The Ambassador said that talks at summit level should be held without any preconditions. I told him that I was not stipulating any condition but only trying to highlight some of the causes which were contributing to the fouling up of the relations between the two countries.

When I reported the substance of my talks with Ambassador Humayun Khan to the Prime Minister, she said that there was no point in resuming talks with Zia when he was persisting in his support for extremists and terrorists not only in Punjab but also in Kashmir. She observed that such a meeting would only serve Zia's objective of getting some international publicity for his "peaceful" intentions. Pakistan's attitude continued to cause her great concern.

Indira Gandhi's sudden visit to Kashmir

On 27 October, Mrs Gandhi suddenly decided to visit Kashmir. She was to visit Orissa on 29 October and there was no previous plan to visit Kashmir before that. She had received reports about the entry of some Pakistan-trained infiltrators into Kashmir and had been quite concerned about it. However, her visit to Kashmir on the 27th was not directly connected with these reports. It was a sudden impulse on her part to visit Kashmir. She enjoyed the visit thoroughly, though it was a very brief one. When I met her on the 28th at her residence, she told me that she wanted to see the *Chinar* trees shedding leaves and it was a sight which had always enchanted her and had she postponed her visit even by a week she would have missed it.

She told me how she went to the market centre at Srinagar without giving any prior notice to the police and how upon recognising her the people in the streets, crowded round her in great joy and excitement. During her stay at Srinagar she had also received reports from some sources about large-scale entry of Pakistani infiltrators into Kashmir and the likelihood of fresh trouble in the area. She sent for General Vaidya and asked him in my presence about the preparedness of the Indian Army to meet any unexpected outbreak of trouble in Jammu and Kashmir. General Vaidya assured her that the Army was well prepared for any eventuality and there was no danger of it being taken unawares by the Pakistanis.

After General Vaidya left, she asked me to remain in close contact with Vice-President Venkataraman and apprise him of her concern at the recent developments in Punjab and Kashmir. She said that it would be helpful to keep him fully informed of all developments and get his views on them. I do not know what prompted her to give me these instructions at that time. Perhaps, she was worried about Pakistan's military intentions in Kashmir and wanted the Vice-President, who was an expert on defence matters, to be kept informed of developments so that she could have the benefit of his advice. I met the Vice-President promptly on the 30th morning and told him about the Prime Minister's concerns

and fears about growing secessionism in Jammu and Kashmii ...
Vice-President explained to me his perceptions about the
preparedness of the defence forces in that region. I also briefed him
on the situation in Punjab and about the problems that had cropped
up in handing over the possession of the Golden Temple to the
control of the priests.

My last meeting with Indira Gandhi

On 29 October, Indira Gandhi left Delhi on a visit to Orissa. She
returned to Delhi at about 8.45 p.m. on the 30th and I met her at
9.10 p.m. in the small living room at her residence at 1 Safdarjung
Road, where I had met her so many times before. This meeting
turned out to be my last one with her. She was still wearing the
same orange coloured saree which she had worn when she made
that prophetic "every drop of my blood..." speech earlier in the
evening at a public meeting in Orissa and which has since become
imprinted in the minds of millions who have watched visuals of
that meeting on television and cinema screens. She looked
unusually tired that night. Indira Gandhi never liked anyone telling
her she looked tired, nor did she ever talk about her feeling tired.
But that night she told me that after her criss-cross journeys by
helicopter and car to many places in the hot weather, she was
feeling very tired.

I also found her somewhat worried. Earlier in the day the car
escorting Priyanka and Rahul was involved in a collision with
another car in Delhi and I thought this incident must have upset
her. Indira Gandhi was never worried about her own safety and had
always dismissed suggestions about strengthening the level of the
security arrangements for her. But she was always worried about
the security of the members of her family, particularly of her
grandchildren. Whatever the reasons might have been, I found her
unusually tired and worried that night and I thought that I should
take only four or five minutes of her time so that she could rest
early. However, the meeting lasted about twenty-five minutes. She
reviewed the Punjab and Kashmir situation with me. There were
some other very important matters on which I had to take her
instructions and thereafter, I informed her while taking leave that I
would be leaving for Bombay early next morning to attend the
meeting of the Atomic Energy Commission. I told her that the

Cabinet Secretary would also be going to Bombay for this meeting.
She then called in R.K. Dhawan and told him that she would not be
attending the office at South Block the next day and all
appointments fixed for her South Block office should be cancelled.
Apparently, she had decided to take it easy on the 31st.

That fateful telephone message

The Cabinet Secretary and I, who were both members of the
Atomic Energy Commission, reached Bombay airport at about 9
a.m. on 31 October and immediately went over to the
Commission's office by helicopter. Ever since the Punjab crisis
started hotting up Rao Sahib and I had an arrangement that we
would not both be absent from Delhi at the same time. We wanted
to ensure that at least one of us must always be available in Delhi to
assist the Prime Minister in dealing with any unforeseen
developments. This was the first time in the last few months that
both of us were being absent from Delhi together.

Raja Ramanna, the Chairman of the Commission, while
welcoming us at the meeting, jokingly remarked that he was very
glad that both the Cabinet Secretary and the Principal Secretary
could be absent from Delhi at the same time and that showed how
peaceful the situation had now become. But Ramanna had spoken
too soon. He had hardly said three or four sentences more by way
of welcome at the meeting when an attendant came in with a
message that there was a very urgent call for me from Delhi. I went
to the adjacent room to take the call. My Personal Assistant from
my office in Delhi was on the line and he said in great panic: "Sir,
I have very bad news. The Prime Minister has been shot a few
minutes ago and taken to the Medical Institute. Her condition is
very critical". I was stunned to hear this. I asked him to repeat
what he had just told me to make sure that I had heard right. He did
so and I listened to these words again with great shock and
disbelief. I then told him to inform everyone concerned that the
Cabinet Secretary and I were rushing back to Delhi. I ran back to
the Committee room and broke the terrible news to those attending
the meeting. Within minutes Ramanna's office arranged a
helicopter for us to go to the airport. I was tormented by the
thought that the President, the Home Minister, the Finance Minister
and Rajiv Gandhi were also away from Delhi, apart from both the

Cabinet Secretary and myself. I cursed myself for having broken our rule. I refused to even consider that the shooting would prove to be fatal. While waiting for the helicopter, we saw a news item on the teleprinter that Indira Gandhi's condition was better and I clung on to that with great hope.

"The worst fears are confirmed"

Cabinet Secretary Krishnaswamy Rao Sahib and I left the office of the Atomic Energy Commission by helicopter for the airport hoping to catch the scheduled Indian Airlines to Delhi, but the plane had left by the time we reached the airport. From the airport we tried to establish contact with Delhi in order to obtain the latest information on Indira Gandhi's condition, but we got nowhere. In fact, nobody in Delhi outside the group of doctors attending on her then knew anything about her condition.

Within minutes, Indian Airlines arranged a special flight to take the Cabinet Secretary and myself to Delhi. Finance Secretary, P.K. Kaul was also with us in the same flight. Throughout that journey, which seemed never-ending to us, we kept trying to get the latest information. Halfway through the flight, the captain came to me and said that the message from Delhi was that "work was in progress". He interpreted this to mean that surgery was going on, and we therefore clung on to the hope that she had survived the attempt on her life. But within half an hour, the captain came again and said to me in a grim voice, "Sir, the message from Delhi is that the worst fears are confirmed". "This", he interpreted, "means that she is no more". The news left us stunned. I just could not reconcile myself with the fact that the vibrant personality who epitomised the strength and stability of the nation and whom I had spoken to only the previous night was no more.

Before landing in Delhi the captain also told us that she had been shot by her own security men.

At the Medical Institute

We reached Delhi airport at about 1 p.m and immediately rushed to the All India Institute of Medical Sciences. Thousands of grief-stricken and anxiety-ridden people had gathered at the Institute but they did not know then that the worst had happened. The news of

Indira Gandhi's death had not yet been announced and even the senior party men and other officials who had managed to get inside the Institute buildings had not been told of it by the doctors in charge.

Upon reaching the eighth floor of the Institute where doctors were still engaged in surgical work on her body, I asked for K.P. Mathur, Indira Gandhi's personal physician. He came out of the operation theatre and tearfully embracing me said that it was all over and that they were now stitching up the body. Rao Saheb immediately left for his office to take charge of the crisis management work. He had to take action on a hundred things in a grave emergency like that. He quickly summoned the senior officers concerned to the Cabinet Secretariat and set up a control room with facilities for receiving information and transmitting instructions very quickly. The crisis management group started working round the clock from the Cabinet Secretariat from that hour. I stayed on at the Institute to attend to the situation there.

By this time, the crowds at the Medical Institute and the roads leading to it had swelled hugely and an atmosphere of frenzy was building up. A large number of senior Congress party men from Delhi and neighbouring states had also managed to reach the eighth floor despite all restrictions imposed by the police. With some difficulty, I got the verandah adjacent to the operation theatre cleared. A room was readied for receiving important visitors and I placed V.S. Tripathi, Joint Secretary in the Prime Minister's Office, to look after the VIPs arriving at the eighth floor. The police thereafter prevented the entry of anyone into the verandah and also to the room next to the operation theatre where Sonia was standing in an utterly anguished condition.

Vice-President Venkataraman arrived at 2.30 p.m. He had come to the Institute earlier in the day and knew that Indira Gandhi was dead. G. Parthasarathi, who had also been there earlier, arrived now. We were now faced with the very strange situation of a vacuum of power. The President was away from the country, though it was reported that his flight was on its way back. With the death of the Prime Minister, her Cabinet also ceased to have any legal authority. Some of the senior members of the Cabinet Committee on Political Affairs, who were also senior in the party hierarchy, like Home Minister Narasimha Rao and Finance Minister Pranab Mukherjee, were out of Delhi. Had they been in

Delhi, at least they could have assumed control of the situation irrespective of their legal status as ministers after the death of the Prime Minister. Most of the Chief Ministers from the Congress-ruled states had by now arrived on the eighth floor of the Institute and began having consultations among themselves. Cabinet ministers, Shankaranand and Shiv Shankar, joined us in the verandah of the operation room.

Brisk consultations started among those present in the verand h on the eighth floor on the question of whether there should be an interim Prime Minister pending the election or a regular successor by the party. The practice on the previous two occasions when the Prime Ministers passed away had been to swear-in an interim Prime Minister. Gulzarilal Nanda was the interim Prime Minister on both the occasions as he had been clearly acknowledged as being the seniormost among the cabinet ministers at that time. Indira Gandhi's cabinet did not have a clearly designated hierarchy but judging by the seating arrangements she had approved for cabinet meetings and for other protocol purposes, Pranab Mukherjee had been informally treated as the seniormost among her cabinet ministers. Therefore, if there were to be an interim Prime Minister, he would have been the one to have been sworn-in. However, there was a strong view among those present at the verandah then that there should be no interim Prime Minister and that Rajiv Gandhi should be sworn-in as Prime Minister immediately upon his arrival in Delhi . The two cabinet ministers present there were quite emphatic in their view that an interim arrangement should be avoided under any circumstance and said that they were opposed to the idea of Pranab Mukherjee being sworn in even for a period of a week.

I moved to the foyer of the eighth floor, where the Congress-I Chief Ministers stood along with some of their ministerial and party colleagues from their states. I talked to Narayan Dutt Tiwari, Chief Minister of Uttar Pradesh, S.C. Mathur, Chief Minister of Rajasthan, Bhajan Lal, Chief Minister of Haryana and J.B. Patnaik, Chief Minister of Orissa, individually and each one of them said that Rajiv should straightaway be sworn in as Prime Minister. They, too, strongly opposed the idea of any interim arrangement. I conveyed their views to those present near the operation theatre and they agreed that a final decision on this issue should be taken after the arrival of Rajiv, who was about to land in Delhi from Calcutta.

Narasimha Rao arrived from Hyderabad and reached the eighth floor at about 3 p.m. I told him the views of the chief ministers and other ministers on the succession and he also said that swearing in Rajiv immediately after his arrival would be the best arrangement.

Rajiv arrived on the eighth floor of the Institute at 3.15 p.m. accompanied by Pranab Mukherjee and Arun Nehru. Anguish was writ large on his face, but he displayed remarkable courage in controlling his emotions. After greeting those of us who were on the verandah, he quickly went into the room adjacent to the operation theatre where Sonia was standing in one corner.

I took Pranab Mukherjee to a corner of the verandah and told him about the views of the senior Congress chief ministers and cabinet ministers about immediately swearing in Rajiv and he said without the slightest hesitation that that would be the best course. There have been some stories that Pranab had staked his claim to be sworn-in as the interim Prime Minister on the basis of earlier precedents and of his seniority in the cabinet, and that he had to be persuaded by others with some difficulty to withdraw his claim. I can state from personal knowledge of what actually happened, that these stories were without any basis. Pranab Mukherjee did not utter even a word against the proposal to dispense with an interim arrangement; on the other hand, he concurred with it wholeheartedly and instantly.

A very serious situation now started brewing in the verandah while Rajiv was inside the room with Sonia. Arun Nehru, who had already talked to G. Parthasarathi, Balram Jakhar and the other senior ministers present took me aside and said that the decision was that Rajiv should straight-away be sworn in as Prime Minister by the Vice-President without waiting for the arrival of the President. He said that he had talked to most of the senior leaders present at the Institute and everyone had agreed with this suggestion. He also said that Rajiv, too, would accept this, though he did not specifically say that he had discussed it with Rajiv and obtained his consent. He said that Zail Singh was already in a hostile mood and he might refuse to swear-in Rajiv without his being formally elected leader by the Congress Parliamentary Party and insist on swearing in the seniormost cabinet minister following old precedents. He said that no such risk should be taken. Any interim arrangement which Zail Singh would make would be of his choice and it was quite clear that his choice would be Pranab

Mukherjee. An interim tenure of Pranab Mukherjee as Prime Minister could cause complications and this should be prevented under any circumstance. On the other hand, if Rajiv was sworn in by the Vice-President before the President landed in Delhi, the President would accept the *fait accompli* even if he did not like it.

I reacted quite strongly against this suggestion. I felt that it would be quite unwise to proceed with this proposal as the President would rightly take it as a clear challenge to his authority and, worse, an indication of a lack of faith in him and, therefore,as an insult. If driven to this position, the President might not accept the validity of the swearing-in by the Vice-President and this would mean very serious legal and constitutional complications.

Much to my surprise, I found that Arun Nehru's proposal had the enthusiastic support of most people present. They were of the view that once Rajiv was sworn in as Prime Minister, the President was unlikely to raise any questions about the validity of the swearing-in by the Vice-President. However, I stood my ground firmly as I felt that this proposal would throw Zail Singh into an open conflict with Rajiv and might lead to a major nation-wide controversy about the legality of the Prime Minister's position. Also, I believed firmly that Zail Singh would swear in Rajiv without raising any objections and there would be no risk in waiting for his arrival. Apart from its impropriety, I was also greatly worried about the constitutional validity of the swearing-in by the Vice-President. The Vice-President could act in the place of the President only in the absence of the President. I said that the President was already on his way back to India and his aircraft could well be over Indian territory even then. It would, therefore, not be legally possible for the Vice-President to perform the functions of the President. I turned to Shiv Shankar, the Law Minister, for his support on my stand who then said, though in a somewhat halting manner, that the legal issue raised by me could not be overlooked. I knew that those pressing for an immediate swearing-in by the Vice-President were doing so out of their anxiety to avoid any complication in the smooth succession of Rajiv. I was perhaps more keenly aware than any one else present there about the strained relationship between Zail Singh and Indira Gandhi. Still, I somehow had the confidence that the President would not raise any objection. At any rate, I felt strongly that it was only proper to wait for his arrival.

back I have often wondered how I took such a strong position against so many important and senior political leaders. I had, in fact, no legal position in the government at that time. With the death of Indira Gandhi I had ceased to be Principal Secretary and had no other official position. Also, I had no position in the Congress Party unlike others who were all important leaders. But these thoughts never entered my mind or in the minds of others present. At any rate, nobody in that group questioned my credentials to express my views in the matter. The only question which Arun Nehru raised, and he raised it very forcefully, was whether those who wanted to await Zail Singh's arrival – meaning me – had any plans ready as to what should be done in case Zail Singh refused to swear-in Rajiv. To that I could only reply that instead of continuing to discuss this issue among ourselves, we should seek Rajiv's decision in the matter.

When everyone agreed that Rajiv's decision on this difficult and rather delicate issue of swearing in should be obtained, Arun Nehru said that he would go inside the room where Rajiv was closeted with Sonia and speak to him. But I said that I would speak to Rajiv myself and went inside the room first.

The scene I witnessed as I moved close to Rajiv was an extremely poignant one. Rajiv was clasping Sonia by both hands in a corner of that room and talking to her very animatedly. Sonia was holding him tightly and with tears rolling down her cheeks was ardently pleading with him not to agree to be Prime Minister. Rajiv was kissing her forehead and trying to convince her that he had to accept the office as it was his duty to do so in that hour of grave crisis. Rajiv saw me standing immediately behind him and knew that I was impatient to talk to him. Time was ticking away and a hundred things had to be attended to after getting Rajiv's decision, and I decided to make an effort to tear him away from Sonia. I whispered to him that I had to talk to him immediately and that the matter was so urgent that I could not wait any longer. He then turned around and came away from Sonia with a gesture indicating to her that he was assuming that she had agreed.

By this time a few women close to the family had entered the room and, finding it difficult to talk to me without being overheard by others, Rajiv took me into the small bathroom attached to it. I mentioned Arun Nehru's proposal to Rajiv very quickly and also the fact that it had been supported by the senior leaders present and my own strong recommendation that it would be advisable to wait till the President arrived and be sworn-in by him. Rajiv immediately agreed with me without the slightest hesitation. He said that the right and proper course was to wait for the President's arrival and to have the swearing-in with his approval, and by him. Rajiv then took Arun Nehru inside the bathroom and himself told him about his preference. What could have developed into a major crisis was thus finally averted by Rajiv's prompt decision. It was about 4.10 p.m. by then and I came out and told those present of Rajiv's decision. Thereupon, we all got busy with the various tasks we had to attend to before the President's arrival.

I have given here an account of this very intimate meeting between Rajiv and Sonia at that dark hour of a great personal tragedy for them after a good deal of hesitation. Normally, I would have avoided any reference to such a strictly personal talk between them, but I was disturbed by certain malicious reports that Sonia had been very keen that Rajiv should become the Prime Minister and had,in fact, pressed him to step into the vacant position. Though such allegations deserve no serious notice, I feel that I owe it to history to place on record what I saw and heard as a witness. I thought a good deal about the propriety of my recording this part of that tragic day's events and came to the conclusion that I would be failing in my duty if I did not do so. The scene of Sonia with tears rolling down her checks, pleading with Rajiv with great emotional fervour not to accept this crown of thorns is one of the poignant memories of that day etched deeply in my mind.

The Congress party leaders present at the Institute decided that the Parliamentary Board of the party should meet immediately at 1 Akbar Road* and pass a resolution nominating Rajiv as the leader of the Congress Parliamentary Party and recommending to the President that he be invited to form the government. News had reached us by then that the President would be coming directly to the Medical Institute from the airport. It was agreed that Narasimha Rao and Pranab Mukherjee should see the President at Rashtrapati

---

* 1 Akbar Road was Mrs Gandhi's office where she somtimes received visitors and held meeting of the Cabinet. 1 Safdarjung Road, next to 1 Akbar Road, was her residence.

Bhavan as soon as he reached there from the Institute and present to him the resolutions of the Congress Parliamentary Board.

The Cabinet Secretary then arrived and we both went into the room where Rajiv was standing by the side of Sonia to ascertain his wishes about the time for the swearing-in ceremony and the other persons to be sworn in as ministers. By this time many more friends and relatives of Mrs Gandhi had arrived and the room became rather overcrowded. Our discussion, therefore, had again to be in the small bathroom attached to the room. Rajiv said that the swearing-in ceremony could be at 6 p.m. subject to the President's convenience and all the members of Indira Gandhi's Council of Ministers should be asked to be present to be sworn in. The Cabinet Secretary returned to his office to make the necessary arrangements, and I went along with Narasimha Rao and Pranab Mukherjee to 1 Akbar Road. Rajiv waited at the Medical Institute to receive the President. The President, immediately on arrival at Delhi airport, expressed his readiness and pleasure to swear-in Rajiv without going through an interim arrangement. That quickly set at rest all doubts on this score. In fact, the President personally informed Rajiv about his decision when he met him at the Institute.

Rajiv sworn-in as Prime Minister

The Congress Parliamentary Board met at 1 Akbar Road and passed resolutions nominating Rajiv as leader of the party and requesting the President to invite him to form the government. All the ministers of Indira Gandhi's cabinet had assembled there and I informed them about Rajiv's instructions that they should be present at Rashtrapati Bhavan at 6 p.m. to be sworn in.

From 1 Akbar Road, P.V. Narasimha Rao, Pranab Mukherjee and I went in the same car to Rashtrapati Bhavan at about 5 p.m. Buta Singh was also following us. We were most unexpectedly confronted at the inner gate leading to the President's office in Rashtrapati Bhavan by an overzealous junior functionary in charge of admitting visitors scheduled to meet the President that evening. He stopped our car abruptly and said we could not go in as we did not have any prior appointment to meet the President. He recognised me sitting in the front seat and also knew that the Home Minister and Finance Minister were in the back seat. But he very casually looked at the papers in his hand and said that he could not

let the car in because our names were not in tl
approved for appointment with the President. I qu
purpose and urgency of our visit, but he was qu
stand. I was already quite tense having had to gu ..
the most agonising and nerve-racking hours of my life that uay.
were also quite pressed for time as the President could proceed
further only after receiving the letter from the Congress
Parliamentary Board. I got out of the car and shouted at the top of
my voice asking him to open the gate immediately for the Home
Minister and Finance Minister to enter, and within a second all his
objections vanished and the gate was opened and we went in.

My immediate task was to draft a resolution of condolence to be
moved at the first meeting of the cabinet. Drafting a resolution on
Indira Gandhi was no easy task, and that too at a time when we
were all so overwhelmed with grief. Still, I hastily wrote out the
resolution and showed it to Narasimha Rao who cleared it after
making a few changes here and there. While we were busy
preparing the documents for the swearing-in function, the Cabinet
Secretary was called to the phone by Rajiv and told that only
Narasimha Rao, Pranab Mukherjee, Shiv Shankar and Buta Singh
were to be sworn-in that day and the others would be sworn-in
later. We had to hastily inform other ministers that they were not in
the first list of ministers to be sworn in.

While the Cabinet Secretary and I were engaged in the
preparatory work for the first Cabinet meeting, the President
accompanied by Rajiv, arrived at Rashtrapati Bhavan, from the
Medical Institute. Narasimha Rao and Pranab Mukherjee
immediately went into the President's room and handed over the
Parliamentary Board's letter to him. The President then formally
conveyed his approval for holding the swearing-in function at the
Ashoka Hall at 6 p.m.

We all assembled at the Ashoka Hall at 6 p.m., but there was a
delay of about forty minutes for the arrival of the President, Vice-
President and the Prime Minister-designate at the Hall. They were
having a discussion among themselves in the President's room. The
swearing-in ceremony was over in ten minutes and we adjourned to
the Cabinet room in Rashtrapati Bhavan for the first meeting of
Rajiv's cabinet.

The first meeting of Rajiv's Cabinet

The first item on the agenda of the cabinet was the condolence resolution. I handed over the draft, which was still in my handwriting, to Rajiv, but he had difficulty in reading my bad handwriting and asked me to read out the resolution. I had a serious problem in controlling my emotions; so had the ministers listening to my reading. Somehow I finished reading those lines and we stood in silence for two minutes.

Indira Gandhi's body was still at the Medical Institute. The Government had yet to make the formal announcement of her death. We had already received a few reports of stone throwing and cars being attacked in some parts of the city. These were indications of the ugly mood of the crowds in the city, though at the time of the cabinet meeting none of us ever imagined that violence and riots would very soon break out on such a large scale.

The cabinet quickly took some important decisions about the cremation. The body was to be brought to 1 Safdarjung Road immediately after the cabinet meeting. It would be moved on the morning of 1st November to Teen Murti House – where Indira Gandhi had spent several happy years as the young hostess in her father's household – and kept there for two days to enable the people to come and pay their last respects. The cremation was fixed for 3rd November at *Shantivan,* the spot where Jawaharlal Nehru had been cremated in 1964.

Immediately after the cabinet meeting, Rajiv left for the Medical Institute to take the body to 1 Safdarjung Road. I went to the crisis management group's office in the Cabinet Secretariat from where Rao Saheb had been directing action on a wide range of administrative and law and order matters to be attended to by the various departments of the central and state governments that night with his characteristic thoroughness and meticulous attention to details.

Indira Gandhi's body at Teen Murti House

I reached 1 Safdarjung Road at 6.30 a.m. on the 1st November. Indira Gandhi's body was kept in the dining room and a small group of women sat around the body singing *bhajans.* The face was surprisingly free of any injury and was still full of serene charm

even though that frail body had taken in several bullets of the
assassins. Entry into the house was restricted to only a few people.

At about 8 a.m. we brought the body to the gun carriage through
the main porch from where she used to leave the house in her white
Ambassador car all these years whether for going to office or for
various other engagements. Now she was leaving on her final
journey through the same porch. Narasimha Rao and Pranab
Mukherjee were with me in the car following the cortege to Teen
Murti House. The body was taken to the main room of Teen Murti
House which faced the porch. The position of the platform on
which it was laid was so arranged that the crowds who were to pass
through the porch could clearly see her face. By this time, there
was a sea of humanity in the premises of Teen Murti House and the
crowds were getting restless and impatient to see the body. Rajiv,
Sonia and the children did their "pranams" to the body first and
others followed. I laid a wreath on behalf of the Prime Minister's
Office and stood by the body's side for a few hours along with
Rajiv and a few others.

Within an hour the crowds at Teen Murti House became
uncontrollable. People appeared to be in a frenzy and the police
and the volunteers found it difficult to introduce even a semblance
of order and discipline. The number became larger by the minute
and many people were close to hysteria. Some of those passing
through the porch were highly distraught with grief and anger and
began raising provocative and inflammatory slogans. At about 11
a.m., we saw some groups of very agitated young men shouting
khoon ka badla khoon ("blood for blood") and shrieking and
gesticulating in wild anger. Thrice Rajiv came out to the porch that
morning to appeal to the assembled people to be calm, and to
chastise those who were shouting such inflammatory slogans.

Army called in at Teen Murti House

At about 1.30 p.m. on the 1st, the crowds in Teen Murti House had
become so unmanageable that there was real danger of their
breaking through the cordon in order to have a closer glimpse of
the body. Some window panes were actually broken and the
situation threatened to become very ugly. We found the police
quite unequal to the task and decided to request the Prime Minister
to call in the Army to take charge of the situation. We also received

reports about attacks on Sikhs and looting of Sikh shops from some parts of the city and of the failure of the Delhi police to deal effectively with the riots. The Cabinet Secretary and I immediately rushed to the Prime Minister's house and suggested that the Army might be called in to take charge of the situation at Teen Murti House and also to deal with the law and order situation in the city. The Prime Minister said that he himself had spoken to the Army Chief, General Vaidya to keep the army in readiness and immediately authorised the calling in of the army.

When the Cabinet Secretary and I reached Teen Murti House, we found the situation there almost out of control. The Army had already started moving to Teen Murti House, but had not yet reached there. The crowds in Teen Murti House appeared to have been seized by a mass hysteria and the police force deployed there was quite unable to keep them under control. Even after the arrival of the troops, it took a good deal of effort and more than an hour to restore order.

At 4.30 p.m. on 1st November, the heads of the foreign missions in Delhi visited Teen Murti House to pay their homage. Rajiv stood by the body to receive their condolences. By this time, several heads of state and other representatives of foreign governments had also begun arriving in Delhi.

On 2nd November, Rajiv received the senior leaders of foreign delegations one by one at 1 Akbar Road. I was with him when Mrs Thatcher, Mr Nakasone, Mr Schulz and other heads of delegations called on him. Mrs Thatcher, dressed in black, was visibly moved when she spoke to Rajiv. She recalled her warm friendship with Indira Gandhi and expressed her sense of personal loss in very touching words. Three former Ambassadors of the U.S. who had known Indira Gandhi very closely – Professor Galbraith, Mr Goheen and Mr Moynihan – called on the Prime Minister together and they spoke with great feeling about their association with Indira Gandhi.

Riots in Delhi and 'shoot at sight' orders

The reports reaching the Control Room in the Cabinet Secretariat about the law and order situation in Delhi had grown increasingly alarming. By the afternoon of 2nd November, the Army had moved into a large part of the city but there were reports from a few places that the police were neither active enough nor effective. The Prime Minister told us on the 2nd afternoon that "shoot at sight" orders should be issued wherever the rioters were indulging in violence. These orders were given wide publicity and had a salutary effect on the situation.

Reports now also started coming in about the outbreak of riots in Uttar Pradesh, Haryana, Bihar, Madhya Pradesh and Jammu. Rajiv went on the air appealing for peace and calm and instructed us to contact the Chief Ministers and Chief Secretaries in all the affected states and to ask them to take the most stringent of steps against the rioters and to prevent the riots from spreading through strong pre-emptive action. Most of the Chief Ministers were in Delhi at this time, but these instructions were conveyed to the Chief Secretaries.

Throughout the night of 2nd November people continued to visit Teen Murti House. It was decided that public *darshan* (viewing) should be stopped at 6 a.m. on 3rd November to make arrangements for preparing the body for cremation.

The Central Government takes over relief work

The riots in Delhi had created a most serious problem of protection and care of the several hundreds of Sikhs, mostly old men, women and children, who had taken temporary shelter in school buildings and several public offices. While the Delhi administration was busy trying to deal with the widespread riots, looting and arson, there were no satisfactory arrangements to look after even the elementary needs of those frightened people who had huddled together apprehensive of renewed attacks and not knowing where to turn to for help. A few camps for refugees had been opened in a purely *ad hoc* manner and hundreds had crowded into such camps which lacked even elementary facilities like electricity, water, food, medicines, etc. Many had seen their close relatives being killed and most did not even have blankets to protect themselves from the biting cold of the Delhi winter. The Delhi administration used all the resources at its command and a few well-intentioned voluntary workers also tried to organise help, but the results were grossly inadequate and the plight of the refugees in these camps had become really desparate.

Mother Teresa arrived in Delhi and started visiting some of these camps in an effort to assess their immediate needs and to organise relief measures wherever possible. The Mother, who knew my wife well telephoned her on the morning of 2nd November and told her that she had found some of the camps to be in a miserable condition and that she was setting out to see the others. Mrs. Pranab Mukherjee and my wife accompanied the Mother on those visits and were quite shocked by the horrible state of affairs they saw in the camps. A few camps had received food and water organised by some groups of citizens who had come forward at great risk to their own lives, but there were several others which had not so far received even drinking water. The Delhi administration's efforts at providing help appeared to have made little impact. Upon recognising Mother Teresa, the refugees in some camps, broke down and begged for drinking water and blankets. In the absence of proper sanitary arrangements, some of these camps had become stinking cesspools of filth.

I received a full account of the condition of the camps from my wife and I reported the state of affairs to the Prime Minister at about 3 p.m. on 2nd November at his residence. He had also received similar reports from groups of his own partymen whom he had deputed to different camps with food, blankets and relief materials. The problems in most camps, however, had become very serious with more and more people crowding into them. Also, newer camps were getting formed as the riots spread. Clearly, the problem had assumed dimensions beyond the capacity of the Delhi administration and of the well-intentioned group of voluntary workers of Delhi.

I told the Prime Minister that the only remedy was for the Central Government to assume direct responsibility for organising relief. The Prime Minister immediately approved the proposal and asked that the resources of all the concerned Central Government departments should be pressed into service. He also directed that the public be informed of the assumption by the Central Government of the direct responsibility for relief work. He said that assistance should reach all the camps that very day and wanted me to report the results of the action taken to him by 9 p.m.

I rushed back to the Cabinet Secretariat and informed the Cabinet Secretary about the blanket authority given by the Prime Minister in organising relief and protection. The Cabinet Secretary immediately formed a Special Action Group of senior officers representing the ministries of Defence, Home, Transport, Health,

Food, Commerce, Civil Supplies, etc., and convened a meeting of this group to plan the relief action. Relief in the form of medicines, water, food, blankets, etc., started flowing into the camps within an hour of the meeting of the Action Group.

The Lt. Governor and the senior officers of the Delhi administration were not too pleased that the central ministries and agencies were stepping into an area which they thought was their responsibility. Their views were ignored and they were told to take instructions from then on directly from the Cabinet Secretary and the Action Group on all matters relating to relief and protection of the sikhs. By 8.30 p.m. that night, practically every camp had been provided with water, food, blankets, medical attention, sanitary arrangements and other such facilities. Wireless communication and security arrangements were made for each camp and senior officers were placed in charge of groups of camps to attend to all emergency needs. Instructions were given to all ministries that all requests for assistance to refugees should be attended to on a top priority without waiting for approval from higher authorities and that whenever necessary financial and administrative clearance should be obtained over the phone; in urgent cases, action should be taken in anticipation of such approval. By about 9 p.m. the Cabinet Secretary and I could report the satisfactory results of this operation to the Prime Minister.

The final journey

3rd November was the day fixed for the cremation at *Shantivan* where a suitable site had already been selected. By early morning, the body had been dressed for the cremation. The Chief Ministers, Governors and other such special invitees who were to join the cortege to the cremation site started arriving at Teen Murti House from 10 a.m. Rajiv, Sonia and their two children arrived by 11 a.m. and went inside the room where the body was kept on a special platform covered with jasmine and roses and remained there by themselves for about fifteen minutes. Thereafter, the President, the Vice-President and other special invitees went inside the room and after offering their respects came out through the main porch and boarded their cars in the appointed order which had been fixed for the journey. The body was then placed on the gun carriage which was pulled by the men of the three armed services. Immediately behind the gun carriage were the three Service Chiefs, Field Marshel Manekshaw, the Chief Justice, the Lok Sabha Speaker, Cabinet Ministers and other important mourners. The Cabinet Secretary, Home Secretary and I followed the cortege in one car for some distance and later peeled off in order to reach the cremation site earlier and look after the arrangements there. As part of the measures to control riots, curfew had been imposed in several places and public transport buses were not operating in most parts of the city. Despite that, thousands of people from Delhi and neighbouring areas had walked long distances and assembled on either side of the roads and at the cremation site.

There were several last-minute arrangements to be attended to before the arrival of the cortege at the cremation site like, proper seating facilities for the foreign delegates and VIPs, and recitation of prayers by priests from different religious denominations. The rush of people in the VIP enclosure was so great that we had to request the Governors and Chief Ministers to leave that enclosure and sit elsewhere in order to accommodate the foreign guests. While waiting for the arrival of the cortege, prayers and devotional songs were recited by priests and representatives of different religions. Mother Teresa also said a few words of prayer which touched the hearts of everyone present. President Zail Singh noticed that there were no *Kirtans* (religious devotional songs) by the sikhs and immediately arranged a group of singers consisting of his daughter and a few others and they recited *Kirtans* in a very moving manner. Darbara Singh, General Sparrow, Buta Singh and others joined in the singing of *Kirtans*.

The cortege arrived at 3.15 p.m. and the body was lifted from the gun carriage and carried on the shoulders of Rajiv and other members of the family to the cremation platform. Rajiv lighted the funeral pyre and within minutes that graceful face which was so familiar to every hamlet and household in India was consumed by sandalwood flames.

For me, personally, a most important chapter in my life had suddenly ended on that fateful morning of 31 October 1984. I told the new Prime Minister the day after his swearing-in that my appointment as Principal Secretary by Indira Gandhi was a personal appointment and I was submitting my resignation to enable him to choose his own Secretary. Later, I gave my resignation in writing but the Prime Minister told me with great warmth and affection that he wanted me to continue. Continuing as Principal Secretary to Rajiv was not much of a change for me, as I had known him well ever since I had joined his mother's secretariat.

On 3rd November, very late in night, the Prime Minister telephoned me on some urgent matter and in an answer to a query, I replied, "Yes, Sir". All these years I had addressed him simply as Rajiv, and this was the first time I was saying "Sir" to him. There was a pause for a few seconds on the other side and then in a somewhat embarrassed tone Rajiv asked me softly, "Dr. Alexander, why did you say 'Sir' to me? You should not be doing that"

I replied: "From the 31st evening you are the Prime Minister and I am your Secretary. I should now address you either as 'Mr. Prime Minister' or 'Sir'. To me 'Mr. Prime Minister' sounds too formal. I would, therefore, prefer 'Sir'".

Again there was a pause at the other end of the telephone and then he quietly continued with the talk. Obviously, Rajiv was accepting the fact that protocol has to have its legitimate place in a Prime Minister's life.

INDEX